GROWTH HACKING: SILICON VALLEY'S BEST KEPT SECRET

CREATIVE. RESOURCEFUL. HIGH-LEVERAGE.

GROWTH HACKING

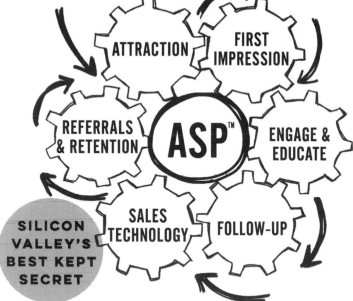

SILICON VALLEY'S BEST KEPT SECRET

RAYMOND FONG & CHAD RIDDERSEN

LIONCREST
PUBLISHING

GROWTH HACKING: SILICON VALLEY'S BEST KEPT SECRET
Raymond Fong & Chad Riddersen

ISBN   978-1-61961-600-4 *Paperback*
        978-1-61961-532-8 *Ebook*

CONTENTS

INTRODUCTION

Imagine growing your business *without* the typical growing pains—no additional staff, no increased work hours, and no more headaches.

When you started out, you envisioned owning a business that spun off cash month after month without you having to work late nights and long weekends. The reality is, when you have the money, you have no time; and when you have the time, you have no money. This dollars-for-hours trade-off cycle is stuck on repeat, and you need a breakthrough in order to achieve your original vision.

Our intention is to show you how to shatter the repeat cycle by reallocating your resources, time and money, in a way that will produce a phenomenal growth result.

Intuitively, the most efficient way to produce a phenomenal result is to replicate someone phenomenal. The thing is, all of your peers are experiencing the same sales results that rise and fall with the economy. Therefore, you need to look beyond your peer group.

The fastest-growing companies in the world are technology start-ups in silicon-monikered regions such as Silicon Valley, Silicon Beach, and Silicon Alley. You've probably heard the stories of twenty-somethings like Palmer Luckey who founded Oculus and sold the company less than two years later to Facebook for a BILLION dollars. From zero dollars to one BILLION dollars in under twenty-four months is unfathomable growth.

Raymond and Chad are growth consultants, also known as "growth hackers," and have worked with some of the fastest-growing companies in the world. They have deconstructed the Silicon Valley playbook and built a framework, the Automated Sales Process™ (ASP™), for any business to replicate and experience Silicon Valley-style growth.

WHAT IS A GROWTH HACKER?

Growth Hacker (noun) /'grōth ha-kər/: *a highly resourceful and creative marketer singularly focused on high-leverage growth.*

Growth hackers thrive in resource-constrained environments where money is tight and time is of the essence. Through a mix of creativity and technology, a growth hacker is able to hack through the jungle, uncover buried resources along the way, and construct the tools needed to grow a business. A growth hacker is the figure-it-out-as-we-go adventurer of Indiana Jones mixed with the problem-solving ingenuity of MacGyver.

Chad Riddersen saw the growth-hacking phenomenon unfold firsthand as a card-carrying member of both the Silicon Valley and Silicon Beach start-up communities. As an investment banker focused on early and growth-stage technology companies, he met with hundreds of entrepreneurs looking to raise millions and sell their company for hundreds of millions. Although several of the companies he worked with were successfully acquired by companies such as Skype, TiVo, and American Express, the vast majority of companies died off or became zombies (dead, but still hobbling along).

What Chad recognized was an emerging pattern that differentiated the successful, rocket-growth companies from the crash-and-burn failures. That pattern was an emphasis on "growth hacking," a term first coined by Sean Ellis in 2010 when looking for candidates to expand the marketing division he headed at the now multibillion-dollar technology company, Dropbox. Sean observed that growth hacking is not something that can be taught in a classroom, but rather it's a mind-set that someone like you can adopt. Distilled down to its core, the mind-set is a singular unrelenting focus on growth.

Chad first observed the incredible power of growth hacking when helping to raise sixty-seven million dollars for LegalZoom, which, at that time, was a company worth half a billion dollars and was less than a decade old. At LegalZoom, the marketing team consisted of an eclectic mix of liberal-arts majors and computer engineers all tasked with one common goal: growth.

Captivated by the mechanics of growing a company, Chad left investment banking to work as a consultant for Dollar Shave Club, a subscription-commerce men's brand that was acquired for one billion dollars cash just four years later. When Chad started working with Dollar Shave Club, they were a couple guys in a shared office in Santa Monica with a shoestring budget going up against the multibillion dollar budgets of razor blade brands like Gillette. How was Dollar Shave Club David going to beat Goliath Gillette selling a product with zero perceivable differentiation? The answer: growth hacking.

Spending $4,500 and filming in a single day, the Dollar Shave Club team created a YouTube video that went viral, racking up over one million views in the first seventy-two hours and bringing in twelve thousand paying customers. While creating viral content is partially attributable to luck, there are certain things that the Dollar Shave Club team did to stack the cards in their favor. Not only was the video launched right before a large industry conference, but the team meticulously scripted comedy tightly woven around the core mission of the company that left viewers chuckling and eager to share with their friends. In a resource-constrained environment where companies mercilessly compete for consumer attention, growth-hacking fortunes favor the creative bold.

Chad was retained a couple weeks after the video went live to help develop the international expansion strategy. Following the completion of the Dollar Shave Club engagement, Chad met Raymond Fong, who had spent years helping small business owners grow, and they reflected, "How can we deconstruct the growth-hacking phenomenon that is enabling tech start-ups to beat out multibillion dollar brands in a way that can be applied to *any* business?"

Raymond had been working with traditional business owners since 2005 as a consultant, trainer, and mentor. He has taught tens of thousands of business owners around the world how to market their businesses online, and he hosted an annual small business conference in Las Vegas that attracted hundreds of entrepreneurs from all across America and beyond. Raymond was no stranger to clever and resourceful online-marketing tactics and had been growth hacking several years before it became a catchy buzzword.

Raymond intimately understood the challenges and tribulations business owners faced when trying to grow their business. Most owners didn't have the working capital to justify traditional marketing efforts where advertising costs were prohibitively high and results were exceedingly slow to bear fruit. By necessity, Raymond had to be creative in his coaching and engineered new ways of achieving the same results as "traditional" marketing channels without the high expense and slow timelines. When Raymond was able to achieve *better* results than the traditional methods, he knew he had engineered something special. After Raymond met Chad, he realized the "something special" he had engineered was what Silicon Valley start-ups were calling growth hacking.

"HOW CAN
WE DECONSTRUCT
THE GROWTH-HACKING
PHENOMENON THAT IS ENABLING
TECH START-UPS TO BEAT OUT
MULTIBILLION DOLLAR BRANDS IN
A WAY THAT CAN BE APPLIED
TO ANY BUSINESS?"

Chad and Raymond's first step was to compile and organize the volumes of blog posts, podcasts, and tech press that detailed the successful application of growth-hacking tactics. There are three case studies you should know about that illustrate the power of and shed light on the hidden history of growth hacking.

Dropbox, the cloud storage company mentioned previously that Sean Ellis was from, cleverly implemented a double-sided incentivized referral program. When you referred a friend, not only did you get more free storage, but your friend got free storage as well (this is called an "in-kind" referral program). Dropbox prominently displayed their novel referral program on their site and made it easy for people to share Dropbox with their friends by integrating with all the popular social media platforms. The program immediately increased the sign-up rate by an incredible 60 percent and, given how cheap storage servers are, cost the company a fraction of what they were paying to acquire clients through channels such as Google ads. *One key takeaway is, when practicable, offer in-kind referrals that benefit both parties.*

Although Sean Ellis coined the term "growth hacking," the Dropbox growth hack noted above was actually conceived by Drew Houston, Dropbox's founder and CEO, who was inspired by PayPal's referral program that he recalled from when he was in high school. PayPal gave you ten dollars for every friend you referred, and your friend received ten dollars for signing up as well. It was *literally* free money. PayPal's viral marketing campaign was conceived by none other than Elon Musk (now billionaire, founder of SpaceX, and cofounder of Tesla Motors). PayPal's growth hack enabled the company to double their user base every ten days and to become a success story that the media raved about. *One key takeaway is that a creative and compelling referral program can not only fuel growth but also generate press.*

Predating PayPal's viral marketing campaign was a growth hack implemented in 1996 by web-based email company Hotmail, which is considered to be one of the first documented growth hacks in the tech community. Hotmail was faced with a massive challenge: their tech peers had huge marketing budgets that they were using to purchase ads on billboards and radio. Hotmail not only had virtually a zero-dollar marketing budget, but they were also giving away their product for free! Billionaire angel investor Tim Draper suggested they should use the email service itself to promote the service by automatically appending "PS: I love you. Get your free email at Hotmail" to the bottom of every message sent through the system. After a bit of resistance, the Hotmail team agreed to do it as long as they didn't have to include the cheesy "PS: I love you" part.

Over the next eighteen months, Hotmail went from zero to twelve million users before being acquired for $395 million. Hotmail's growth hack was so successful that Apple copied it a decade later with the launch of the iPhone, where every email sent on the device would automatically say, "Sent from my iPhone," at the bottom. *One key takeaway is that there is no shame in swiping a growth hack that has worked for someone else and applying it to your business, Apple built one of the most valuable businesses in the world doing it.*

At first glance, it may seem that the tactics of tech companies like Dropbox, PayPal, and Hotmail have little relevance to your business, but we dug deeper and uncovered a huge treasure trove of growth hacks, and all it takes is one well-executed hack to revolutionize your business. Most importantly, we constructed a clear framework for you to organize and prioritize the growth tactics: the Automated Sales Process™ (ASP™).

In the process of learning about growth hacking, you will find recognizable analog to digital (a.k.a. offline to online) parallels that transfer what you already know about marketing to a clear digital marketing framework, the ASP™. Simultaneously, we will be reprogramming your mind-set

"

...WE CONSTRUCTED A CLEAR FRAMEWORK FOR YOU TO ORGANIZE AND PRIORITIZE THE GROWTH TACTICS: THE AUTOMATED SALES PROCESS™ (ASP™).

so you are thinking with the technological creativity of a growth hacker. Once you know what is possible with technology, you will begin to conceive clever growth hacks with a degree of creativity you never knew you had.

Before we begin, it must be noted that the growth hacks detailed in the case studies above were merely modern renditions of old-school marketing tactics. Earl Tupper, the founder of Tupperware, perfected referral marketing way back in the 1950s. Additionally, Conrad Gessner used word-of-mouth advertising tactics to make tulip bulbs "go viral" back in the 1500s. Gessner's viral marketing culminated in what is now known as "Tulipmania," where the price of a tulip bulb commanded the modern day equivalent of $1 million. You will be pleasantly surprised to find that most growth-hacking tactics are simply technological implementations of marketing strategies that have existed for centuries.

AVERAGE IS OVER

Given that you picked up this book, it's clear that you are mentally prepared for change, and change is the first step. When faced with the typical challenges of growing a business, the average business owner is going to try to work longer hours...and then burn himself out; hire more staff... and then sacrifice profitability; invest in more overhead... and then not get a return on investment.

You are NOT the average business owner. You embrace change and are motivated by the pursuit of happiness and, ultimately, freedom. Your path to freedom is to learn how to hack growth; your path to learning how to hack growth is through the collective knowledge of those who have hacked growth before you; and your path to knowledge starts by reading this book.

GROWTH HACKING YOUR MIND

Growth hacking is a new way of thinking. As with anything new, our natural first reaction is to be skeptical. Our conscious and subconscious selves are conditioned to fight the unknown by reverting safely back to the status quo. After all, the status quo is what's familiar to us; it's what we are comfortable with.

Comfort is a death sentence to progress, and progress is what you seek.

Before you growth hack your business, you must first hack your mind. Your previous experience has created deeply entrenched pathways that produce your current realm of perceived possibility. You need to trench new pathways so that you can make new connections and discover new opportunities. The pick and shovel you need to dig new neural pathways are a set of core beliefs that will rewire the way you think and empower you on your path to progress.

BECOMING RESOURCE RICH

Your two primary resources come in the form of time and money. The challenge you are likely facing is that you do not have a surplus of either resource. While at first this may seem like a disadvantage, the reality is that all of your competitors face the same challenge. Most business owners use the lack of resources as an excuse, saying, "I'll do Y when I have X amount of money saved," or "I'll do Y when I have X amount of free time." As a savvy and self-aware business owner, accept that you will never have X extra money or free time. Your competitive advantage will come from your ability to intelligently *reallocate* your scarce resources to achieve breakthrough growth.

Most business owners are too afraid to invest more resources on growth because it requires you to sacrifice short-term profitability. As with most things we are afraid of, your fear festers in the void of the unknown. Most companies don't track their finances close enough to know how much they can even spend on growth (and no, finding out how much you spent on growth when you do your taxes doesn't qualify as "close enough"). Of the companies that do track their finances close enough (usually on a monthly or quarterly basis), most have no benchmark to determine how much is "too much" or "too little" to spend on growth. So, your first step to fracture the fear of investing more resources on growth is to track your finances on a monthly or quarterly basis. Your second step is to benchmark your growth against the right metric. Continue reading for guidance on what to benchmark against.

While it may appear on the outside that Silicon Valley's fastest-growing companies achieve growth by having a "really good idea," there are plenty of companies that have great ideas and fail. What differentiates the fastest-growing companies from their peers is that they're not afraid to invest a massive amount of resources on growth.

We analyzed the ten tech companies worth over a billion dollars that went public in 2014 and 2015, and the average company spent a jaw-dropping $0.72 on sales and marketing for every $1.00 of sales during the three-year hypergrowth period before going public. As a matter of fact, one of the companies, Box, spent $1.59 for every $1.00 in sales!

You're probably wondering, how does a company like Box justify spending more money on sales and marketing than they generate in sales? The answer is "customer lifetime value." Once Box mathematically proved that they could acquire a customer for less than the lifetime value (LTV) of that customer, they raised a war chest of investment capital and didn't care if they spent more on sales and marketing than they generated in annual sales, because they knew that they would generate a big return in the long run.

You probably don't have access to a massive war chest of investment capital, but that doesn't mean you are unable to invest more resources on growth. Instead of benchmarking your growth investment against customer lifetime value, benchmark against your bottom-line profits. Here is a list of financial scenarios and corresponding actions:

- If you desire growth and have a profitable business, operate at a break-even point and reinvest the profit, or a portion of the profit, back into growth.
- If you are running a break-even or unprofitable business, spend some time going through your expenditures looking for redundancies or unnecessary expenses.
- If you cannot find any opportunities to save money, prepare yourself to take a temporary pay cut (you can time this around your tax refund or right after your busy period if your business has seasonality).
- If you are unable to take a temporary pay cut, prepare yourself to work some extra hours (start by batching activities so you can spend a day per week working from home, and use the time you save when not having a work commute to invest in growth).
- If you are unable to take a temporary pay cut AND unable to work any extra hours, then read the paragraph below.

If you have no time or money, then you need to focus on "life hacking" before you start growth hacking. While there are volumes of books and articles written on life hacking, the common thread is the maximization and optimization of your energy, both mental and physical. We curated some of the most simple, relevant, and impactful life hacks as follows:

- **Write things down.** Think of your brain as a computer. If you have a bunch of programs open, your computer will start to slow down. Close your mental "programs" by saving things onto a "hard drive" by writing things down.

- **Choose essentials.** Once you have written what's floating around in your mind down ask yourself, what one thing, if done today, will make all other things easier or irrelevant?

- **Visualize.** Once you have written down your one thing, visualize your ideal day, and focus on accomplishing that one thing. Think of this as clearing out your mental cobwebs so you can think clearly.

- **Organize: morning vs. evening.** Do your one thing early in the day when you have the greatest amount of mental energy. Save "low bandwidth" administrative tasks for later in the day when you are running low on mental energy and less likely to focus on your one thing.

- **Avoid switching costs.** Unlike a computer, your brain cannot switch from task to task on a moment's notice. Switching requires your brain to consume extra energy trying to recalibrate and find the point where you last left off. In this regard, your brain is like a car, it takes a lot of energy to get up to cruising speed, but once it gets to cruising speed, it doesn't take a lot of energy to stay there. Multitasking sounds great, but in reality, it consumes more energy, so focus on one thing at a time.

- **Be healthy.** You already know that sleep, diet, and exercise will help you live a healthier and longer life. While

> **COMFORT IS A DEATH SENTENCE TO PROGRESS, AND PROGRESS IS WHAT YOU SEEK.**

getting *more* sleep and *more* exercise takes *more* time, improving your diet does not. Improve the fuel you put into your body, and capitalize on the benefits the increase in energy provides you.

In a scenario where you have no time and no money, you must hack your body and mind to boost your energy and increase the output from the time you do have. The additional output will be in the form of increased productivity that, assuming you are accomplishing that one thing you establish every day, will translate into more money. Congratulations, you have broken the stuck-in-a-rut cycle, and you are ready to start growth hacking your business.

TECHNOLOGY SKILLS NOT REQUIRED

If you are technologically inclined, you are welcome to skip to the next section. If you are NOT a technologist, there are many ways to turn this into a growth-hacking advantage. Too many hardcore technologists are constrained by what they *believe* to be possible based on their past experiences. On the other hand, if you are not technology savvy, you are not susceptible to this common self-limiting belief. You are free to dream up new technology solutions and flirt with what many technologists would falsely deem unreasonable. After all, great technological advancements in the world were not conceived by men who operated in a world of constraints and limitations. They were conceived by men who dared to be bold.

As a nontechnologist, you can commission a hardcore technologist to build tools for you. Once you see some examples of the technology that Silicon Valley growth hackers are using, you will recognize that virtually anything is possible. Unrestrained by the knowledge of what technology already exists, your thinking will inevitably be more outside the box.

Once you have conceived a technology solution, you must make sure to do your diligence in order to avoid, proverbially, reinventing the wheel. Many hackers are infected by the desire to build everything from scratch without fully researching what off-the-shelf solutions are available. Make sure you research online and talk to people with a solid grasp of technology before concluding that no current technology exists. More than likely, there will be another technology solution that, even if it isn't built specifically for your use-case, can be repurposed and recalibrated to solve your problem.

To give you comfort, Apple cofounder Steve Jobs didn't know how to code. By asking questions and challenging the status quo, Jobs embodied the mantra of thinking differently, and his results speak for themselves.

Just because you do not know how to code does not mean you cannot hack growth. Growth hacking does not necessarily need to be embodied in a single individual. It can be a mentality adopted and executed by the collective skill sets of a group. In other words, sometimes marketing and technology skills are possessed by one person, and other times, one person is the marketer and the other is the technologist. As long as the group is communally focused on growth, the results will be the same (if not better).

THE FIELD OF DREAMS FALLACY

The single, most limiting core belief we rewire for business owners is the false hope that "if I provide an excellent product and service to the market, everything else will take care of itself." We call this limiting core belief the "Field of Dreams fallacy," paying homage to Kevin Costner's classic film that popularized the mantra "if you build it, they will come."

The present-day reality is, "if you build it, they won't just come."

The reason the Field of Dreams fallacy is so commonplace is because there was a time in history when it wasn't a fallacy. In an environment with no competition, when there was only one business in town that did X, if you

> APPLE COFOUNDER STEVE JOBS DIDN'T KNOW HOW TO CODE. BY ASKING QUESTIONS AND CHALLENGING THE STATUS QUO, JOBS EMBODIED THE MANTRA OF THINKING DIFFERENTLY, AND HIS RESULTS SPEAK FOR THEMSELVES.

did X, customers had to come to you. But you are now operating in a hypercompetitive market with plenty of companies that provide competing solutions. In order to be found first, you need to market yourself.

THE WHY THAT MAKES YOU CRY

What motivates you to grow your business? The surface-level motivator is likely financial, but money, by definition, is simply an instrument used to store value. We want you to go one level deeper and identify what you intend to exchange that store of value for. Do you want to retire and leave a legacy for your children? Is there a dream home that you want to build? Is there a bucket list of activities and destinations you want to experience? Once you identify what money ultimately enables for you, visualize achieving that and connect an emotion with that visualization. For many, the feelings of achievement conjure up a teary-eyed emotion and for others, a feeling of blissful elation. Once you have introspectively struck this cord in your heart, take a moment to write down your "why that makes you cry" in the space provided on the following page.

WRITE DOWN THE "WHY THAT MAKES YOU CRY"
IN THE SPACE PROVIDED HERE

The personal "why that makes you cry" is the subconscious fuel for your soul that is essential for your long-term success. Money is merely a byproduct of your ability to provide value to the world and simply an intermediary between your efforts today and what your efforts unlock in the future.

Given that you are in the process of developing your inner growth hacker, one of the best motivational growth hacks is to establish a "why that makes you cry" on a personal *and* professional level. You already established your personal motivation. On a professional level, how does the product or service you provide add value to the people you provide it for? For example, the Ford Motor company doesn't sell automobiles; they sell freedom and independence. Costco doesn't sell bulk goods; they sell the opportunity to save money and provide for your family. Disney doesn't sell movies; they sell an imaginative escape from the daily grind. What do you sell? How are you helping the world? Why are you in business in the first place?

Never lose sight of your "why." This will keep you pushing forward when you want to cave back into complacency.

THE PRESENT-DAY REALITY IS, "IF YOU BUILD IT, THEY WON'T JUST COME."

HOW TO GET THE MOST FROM THIS BOOK

You own this book; this book does not own you. Take fifteen minutes, scan the Table of Contents, skim the headlines, review the graphics, and read the conclusion. If anything piques your interest when reviewing the Table of Contents, read the introduction and concluding takeaways in those chapters. If you are hungry for more, read some of the supporting information in the body paragraphs.

If you are the type of reader who likes to soak up every word, but you don't feel as if you have the time right now, get the audio version or e-book (if you haven't already). If you have a good ear, listen to the audio version on twice the speed while you are commuting. If you buy the e-book, download it on your phone so you can read it when you are stuck in line at the grocery store. Our intention is to teach you how to think like a growth hacker, and hacking the way in which you consume the information in this book is an excellent place to start developing your new skill set.

What you are about to read is the distillation of our more than ten thousand hours of growth hacking and the founding concept behind our growth-hacking consultancy, Deviate Labs, where we have worked with countless entrepreneurs exactly like yourself.

Now, get ready for growth-hacking enlightenment.

ESTABLISHING AN AUTOMATED SALES PROCESS (ASP™)

The grandson of the founder of one of Seattle's first auto body shops approached us to help turn around sales that had been in a slow, unrelenting decline for nearly a decade. The grandson had watched the legacy his grandfather built and father maintained start to erode away as dozens of competing auto body shops opened up in the local area. Despite being only twenty-three years old, he inherited control of the business that was surviving on borrowed money, six months away from bankruptcy, and in dire need of immediate and dramatic change.

His grandfather and father had an aversion to advertising and had relied on word-of-mouth marketing to grow. The grandson was perceptive to observe that the word-of-mouth conversation had moved online, and he recognized that the shop's digital presence was lackluster to say the least. We moved at lightning speed to implement the ASP™ and took the digital presence from lackluster to best-in-class in a matter of months.

Within the year, the auto body shop went from being one of the many auto body shops in town to "the" auto body shop in town. Business boomed as new, high-quality customers filled the auto shop. As a testament to transformation, the company was approached by an American manufacturer of luxury electric cars to pilot a new repair program in the Seattle area. How do you think this major manufacturer found their shop amid all the auto body shops in Seattle? You guessed it: through the ASP™.

This is merely one of the many examples of astonishing results attributable to the implementation of an ASP™.

ASP™ DECONSTRUCTED

The quickest way of understanding an ASP™ is by way of analogy. Think of an ASP™ as a digital replica of the perfect salesperson. The perfect salesperson will naturally attract prospects, set a polished first impression, keep prospects engaged as well as educate them, follow up with them at just the right time and handle any objections with expert salesmanship, skillfully close the sale while simultaneously looking for upsell opportunities, and get referrals while retaining them as customers for life. Whether your top salesperson is you or someone on your team, that person will inevitably have a bad day, take vacations, and need benefits. The ASP™ takes the perfect version of your sales process and permanently stamps it into a technology system that works for you 24/7/365, never having a bad day, never needing a vacation, and never requiring benefits.

The ASP™ is the growth-hacking framework we implement for our clients that range from traditional brick-and-mortar businesses to venture-backed technology start-ups. It's a framework that can be applied to any type of business, and in the next several chapters, we'll dive into ASP™ and its six individual components and show you how to best implement them for your business.

THE SIX ASP™ COMPONENTS

1. Attraction
2. First Impression
3. Engage & Educate
4. Follow-Up
5. Sales Technology
6. Referrals & Retention

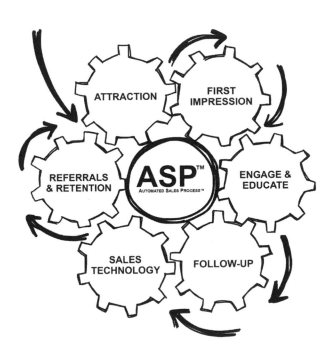

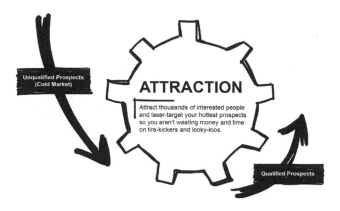

1. ATTRACTION

Attraction is the means of getting attention for your products and services. In the offline world, Attraction consists of TV, print, radio, and word-of-mouth marketing, among the many others you are familiar with. Each offline channel has an online parallel: TV = YouTube, print = website display ad, radio = online radio, word-of-mouth marketing = social media sharing. Just like offline, there are different flavors within each channel. For example, in the offline world, print ads range from billboards to benches, and in the online world display ads range from pay-per-click ads to pop-ups. While the tactics may vary, the goal remains the same: get attention.

The Attraction component works to eliminate marketing resource waste by quickly parsing through unqualified, cold-market prospects and pulling out prospects that are qualified for your product or service with targeted advertising.

In the chapter dedicated to Attraction, we will detail the unique benefits that online marketing possesses: analytics, attribution, and automation. Moreover, we will walk through a thought exercise that will help you train your mental growth-hacking muscle and, in the process, uncover specific tactics you can immediately apply to your business.

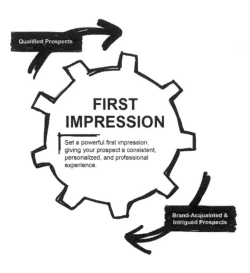

2. FIRST IMPRESSION

Once you've attracted your qualified prospects, you want to ensure that you make a good first impression by giving your prospects a consistent, personalized, and professional experience. In the offline world, your first impression is established when someone walks into your office or storefront. In an online world, your first impression is established when someone visits your website or stumbles upon your presence on social media.

The aim of the First Impression component is to turn your qualified prospects acquired via the Attraction component into brand-acquainted and intrigued prospects.

In the First Impression chapter, we will give you a framework for how to prioritize your investment and ensure a return.

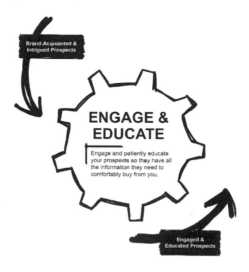

3. ENGAGE & EDUCATE

When you've made a favorable impression on your potential client, the next step of the ASP™ is to engage and educate that potential client about your product or service. In the offline world, there are subtle psychological tricks that influence visitors to take specific actions. For example, a warmly lit and Wi-Fi enabled lounge area at your local coffee shop encourages you to stay until your stomach begins to grumble and you find yourself buying an overpriced muffin you passed on when you first purchased your latte. In an online environment, there is an equal amount of subtle psychological tricks that will encourage your visitors to take certain sales-producing actions.

The Engage & Educate component transforms brand-acquainted and intrigued prospects into an engaged and educated prospect that is much more likely to trust you, like you, and ultimately do business with you.

In the Engage & Educate chapter, we will walk through the nine subcomponents of the subconscious sales system.

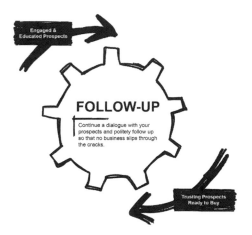

4. FOLLOW-UP

In even the most scientifically designed subconscious sales system, the vast majority of visitors will not purchase from you immediately. The path to real riches rests in the follow-up. In the offline world, follow-up activities range from phone calls to mailing lists, but these are often forgotten or neglected because they take a significant amount of time, money, and attention. The online follow-up environment has a set-it-and-forget-it quality that makes it sustainable and incredibly lucrative.

The Follow-Up component effortlessly converts engaged and educated prospects into trusting prospects that are ready to buy, whether that's today or at a later time.

In the Follow-Up chapter you will discover a personalized, nonintrusive, and automated way of continuing a dialogue with your prospects that ensures that when they're ready to buy, they think of you first.

5. SALES TECHNOLOGY

When your prospect is ready to buy, it's your role to move them through a frictionless sales experience that shepherds them smoothly to the point of purchase. In the offline world, point-of-purchase tactics range from conveniently crafted upsells, to offering a wide variety of payment options, to gifting a complimentary breath mint. Believe it or not, it's possible to replicate these point-of-purchase tactics in an online environment. Moreover, in an online environment your business will no longer be

encumbered by human constraints when closing a sale. You can book appointments, take payment, and recommend upsells at 2:00 a.m. on a Saturday.

The Sales Technology component of the ASP™ is where the magic happens, converting your trusting prospects to paying customers.

In the Sales Technology chapter, we will help you design a suite of sales technology to perform a set of technology tasks that you never knew were possible.

6. REFERRALS & RETENTION

Once you have closed the sale, as you know, the sales process is not over. The final step is to ask for referrals and retain that customer for life. In the offline world, asking

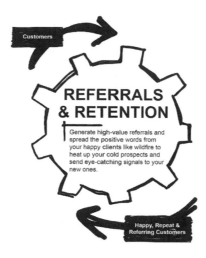

REFERRALS & RETENTION

Generate high-value referrals and spread the positive words from your happy clients like wildfire to heat up your cold prospects and send eye-catching signals to your new ones.

for a referral may be as simple as leaving your business card, and retention may consist of a customer-appreciation gift at the end of the year. In the online world, your business card can be replaced by a prepopulated social media post, and a gift can be credited instantaneously to your happy customer's account the moment one of his or her friends becomes a customer. The reach and instant gratification that technology generates is unparalleled.

The Referrals & Retention component influences one-off customers into becoming happy, repeat, and referring customers.

In the Referrals & Retention chapter, we will show you how to build an automated and incentivized system that doesn't lose the personal touch.

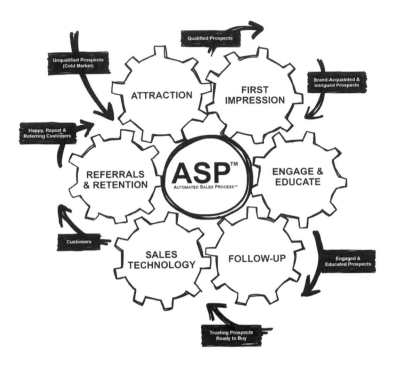

The ASP™ is a cyclical process, transforming unqualified, cold-market prospects into happy, repeat, and referring customers. Much like an engine's flywheel, a well-engineered ASP™ produces self-propelling referral momentum that fuels more prospects into the system. Continuing with the engine analogy, as you gain familiarity of the component parts in the subsequent chapters, you will identify ways to hack and modify the engine to tailor it for your business and maximize your performance. In the end, the value of the entire ASP™ will be far greater than the sum of the value of each component part.

WHY AN ASP™?

Most business owners get lost in the tactical weeds, losing sight of the strategic forest. You've had marketing gurus tell you that "you need be posting more on Facebook." You've read tip-of-the-day business articles proclaiming that "you need to start using negative keywords to optimize your AdWords spend." You've been told by colleagues that "you need to start buying leads from XYZ lead generation service." Frankly, no one tactic is bad or wrong. The problem is, you are drinking from the fire hose of isolated tactics without having any framework, mental model, or context to prioritize, organize, and assess the applicability to your situation. The ASP™ is your strategic compass that will enable you to navigate to prosperity instead of drowning in a sea of tactics.

The ASP™ is most powerful when fully implemented, but you do not need to build all six components at once to reap the benefits. Each component can be built and improved on one by one. For example, you don't need to preoccupy yourself with improving your first impression if you aren't attracting many prospects in the first place. The high-level understanding of the ASP™ framework that you have developed so far may now enable you to identify certain bottlenecks in your current sales process that you can drill down on. For example, you may recognize a weakness on Referrals & Retention and prefer to skip ahead to that chapter. The point we are making is that the ASP™ is purposefully designed as a mental model to empower you to hack through all the tactic-filled noise and focus on implementing the strategic signal.

THE REWARDS OF AN ASP™

While the reasons and rewards of having an ASP™ vary person to person, we want to share a few examples as inspiration for what you are about to achieve:

ASP™ INSPIRATION

- After nearly doubling his sales in twelve months, one of our clients was able to finally afford the best health care for his ailing wife and spend more time as a couple traveling in the Bahamas.
- After several quarters of more than 30 percent growth, another client of ours paid for their children and grandchildren's travel and accommodation expenses for a ten-day reunion at a twelve-bedroom mansion in Lake Tahoe.
- After transforming a struggling company into a burgeoning business, a son was able to afford his father the opportunity to proudly retire after building the family business for thirty years.
- After nine months of record-breaking growth, a husband-wife team was able to afford the absolute best private school for their three children.

It brings us an immeasurable amount of joy to be able to share with you the secrets that have enabled Silicon Valley's tech elite to accumulate an inordinate amount of wealth over such a short period of time. We have taken Silicon Valley growth-hacking tactics and applied them to businesses like yours for several years. Through trial and error, we have developed and fine-tuned a framework, the ASP™, so that growth hacking can be applied to *any* business. We have been able to replicate success time and time again with our consulting clients, and now we have made this knowledge available to you so that you can grow without the typical growing pains, achieve your dreams, and leave behind a legacy.

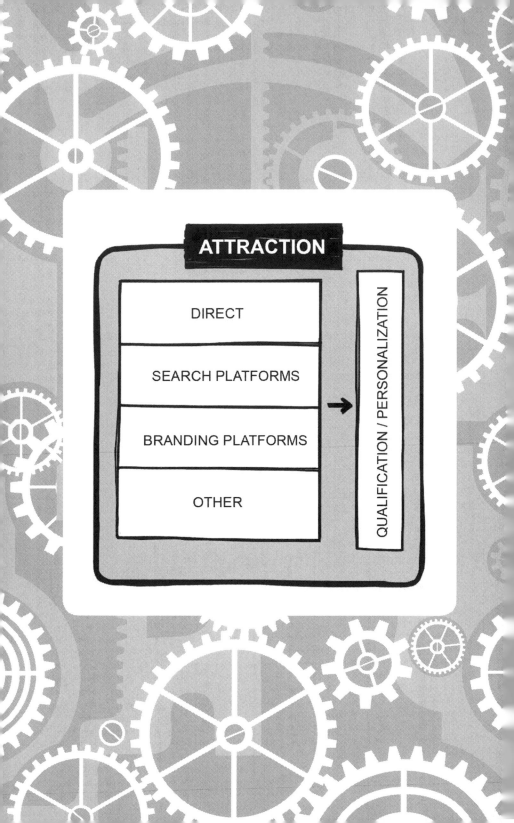

ATTRACTION

Attract thousands of interested people and laser-target your hottest prospects so you aren't wasting money and time on tire-kickers and looky-loos.

If you had a chance to pitch your product to seven *million* people hanging on your every word, your sales would automatically explode through the roof, right?

That's exactly what our soon-to-be client thought as he landed a feature spot on ABC's hit prime-time TV show *Shark Tank*.

In anticipation of being on America's most popular business show, he accumulated a massive stockpile of inventory. Not only was there going to be thousands of orders to fulfill from the seven-million-person audience, but the Sharks were going to introduce him to enormous big-box retailers that were going to place huge whole-sale orders.

Or so he thought...

When the show aired, our soon-to-be client invited all his friends, family, and coworkers over to his house to celebrate the monumental occasion. He even had his laptop perched in front of him during the show so he could watch the orders roll in in real-time.

When he first appeared on screen, he didn't see any orders come in, so he refreshed his inbox. No new orders.

He thought there was probably a slight delay, so he waited sixty seconds and refreshed his inbox again. One order.

Okay, things were probably just delayed, but only one new order was slightly concerning. He had thought there would be thousands by now.

When the show ended, he sold less than a hundred units and was in disbelief.

Not only was the situation disappointing from a business

perspective, but he felt embarrassed in front of his friends, family, and coworkers.

The company was at an absolute low. There was no money because it had all been spent stockpiling inventory. There was no Rolodex of connections from the Sharks because they had all passed on the investment opportunity. With his back against the wall, he approached us to hack growth and attract the right audience that would appreciate the unique product.

THE DATA DIFFERENCE

What differentiates attracting prospects online versus offline is the availability and abundance of data. Data creates a feedback loop for your marketing to help you continually fine-tune what you say, how you say it, and where you say it. John Wanamaker, a New York City department-store owner living one hundred years ago, lamented, "Half the money I spend on advertising is wasted; the trouble is, I don't know which half." While this sentiment is true of the traditional offline advertising methods Mr. Wanamaker was pursuing, this is absolutely NOT true of the online advertising methods a growth hacker pursues.

Advertising online gives you unprecedented control that

many take for granted or overlook entirely. If you told John Wanamaker that one hundred years from now he could show an ad for his custom-tailored suits exclusively to thirty- to forty-nine-year-old males located in a ten-mile radius of his department store with household incomes greater than $75,000 and who work in finance, he would have looked at you in jaw-dropping disbelief. Not only can you serve the ad to someone who possesses the exact characteristics of your ideal buyer, but you can track the specific ad that person clicked on to go to your website, review the webpages he viewed, and determine whether or not he decided to purchase from you. This immediate attribution and feedback loop of online advertising empowers you to know which half of your advertising is wasted so you may eliminate the waste.

Another key data-enabled difference between online and offline advertising is the ability to start small and scale up. For a couple dollars per day, you can start running ads online with the freedom to cease any time you please. Comparatively, offline channels, such as print, require upfront fees and minimum circulation commitments while taking months for your ad to get into the hands of prospective buyers. When you identify an online ad that is producing buyers, you can quickly scale it up as the ad inventory is available on demand. When you identify an offline ad that is producing buyers, you must wait until the next advertising cycle to scale it up, which could be months away. The opportunity to start small and scale quickly is one of the founding principles of the growth-hacking gospel and the reason why online advertising is such a uniquely powerful medium.

The final data-enabled difference between online and offline advertising is the ability to automate. We worked with a financial service client that decided to staff from 8:00 a.m. to 12:00 p.m. on Saturday, and they wanted us to drive leads for their call center to field. So we set up an online advertising system that automatically served ads for those specific times on Saturday. Once it was 12:00 p.m., the system would shut off until 8:00 a.m. Monday morning, when people were back in the office to field sales calls. This technique is referred to as "day-parting," and it exemplifies only one of many ways that your online advertising may be automated. The ability to automate your advertising in this manner is something that simply does not exist in the offline world.

The intention is not to say that traditional advertising methods are bad, but rather to illustrate the difference and underscore the benefits of digital advertising methods. Many growth hackers overlook the fact that the average person still spends more time engaging with nondigital media (TV, radio, print, and so on) than digital media in the average day. Although the digital-media balance will slowly exceed that of nondigital, it will take a generation or two before nondigital is NOT a material source of time spent. As of this writing, the average American spends a collective twelve hours per day exposed to media, and more than half of that is traditional TV, radio, print, and other nondigital formats.

While the initial out-of-pocket expense may be low, advertising inventory scalable, and ad serving automatable for online attraction, there is a certain time when an adept growth hacker should pursue offline opportunities as well. We will explore this more in the Advertising Arbitrage section.

THE AVATAR

In an offline advertising environment, businesses tend to focus on maximizing reach based on the guiding principle that more eyeballs generate more customers. In an online advertising environment, maximizing exclusively for reach will get you into trouble. Online, you need to optimize for precision, identifying the exact audience you want to market to. This process starts with identifying your "avatar."

As we talked about in the preceding section, there is an

abundance of data available online, which allows for an unfathomable degree of precision. In the offline advertising world, you target audiences based on general geographic and broad demographic information. For example, we ran a radio ad for a roofing contractor client, knowing that the contractor serviced only a portion of the folks in that broadcast region and that only a portion of the listeners owned a home. In contrast, thanks to social media platforms such as Facebook, there are hundreds of demographic data points at your disposal that you can use to your advantage. The growth hack used by Silicon Valley tech companies to parse through and organize the multitude of digital demographic data is to create an avatar, a digital representation of your ideal buyer.

The challenge with having an abundance of demographic information is that it's easy to get overwhelmed. The avatar humanizes the data deluge as a representative and comprehensible person. The avatar also becomes the test dummy for your marketing strategies and angles. If you don't think the avatar would resonate with your marketing, then you need to change your approach.

Here are some questions to ask yourself when developing the perfect avatar. Keep in mind that you may have multiple avatars because there are likely multiple versions of the ideal buyer, but start with the most important one.

AVATAR FORMATION QUESTIONS

What gender is your ideal buyer?

How old is he or she?

What's his or her profession?

What's his or her annual income?

Where does he or she live?

Is he or she married?

Does he or she have kids?

What are his or her hobbies?

What are his or her interests?

A popular Silicon Valley advertising mantra is that demographics don't buy products; people do. Your avatar is the digital representation of that person that all marketing should cater to.

FIRST WHO, NOW WHAT?

Once you have established your avatar, the next step is to determine when, where, and how to reach those ideal buyers. The determination is as easy as putting yourself in your avatar's shoes, but there are several slippery slopes and sand traps that you need to watch out for.

Regarding *when*, focus first on when your avatar is in a buying mood or most likely to take a buying action. One of the clearest indicators of buying action is the keywords the avatar uses when performing an online search. Continuing with the roofing contractor example, we didn't advertise to everyone who was searching for "roofing" online, but we focused on people searching for terms such as "new roof," "fix a roof leak," "roofing contractor." These terms signify that the person is in a position to spend money on hiring a roofing contractor.

Once we exhausted the ad inventory with purchase intent, we expanded to people considering investing in a solution but who need more information before deciding. For example, many people search for things like "What are the benefits of a composite roof?" Although their search doesn't indicate immediate purchase intent, when exposed to the rest of the ASP™, we can lead them to a purchase decision.

Once we exhausted the ad inventory with education interest, we expanded to folks who are aware of their problem but may not be in a position to actively solve that problem. For example, we served display ads to homeowners on Facebook touting the benefits of having your roof inspected before the rainy season.

In summary, focus on purchase intent, then education-based interest, and then awareness-based interest when reaching out to your avatar.

Regarding *where*, focus on where your avatar spends time. Once you have clearly defined your avatar, this should be a much easier exercise. For example, if your avatar is a forty-five-year-old housewife, you would focus on widely adopted social platforms. If your avatar is a fifty-five-year-old male, you would focus on certain news publications. If your avatar is a fifteen-year-old teenager, you would focus on newly created social apps.

Whether you determine where your avatar spends time by intuition or analysis, the *where* will feed into your determination of *how* to reach your avatar.

Regarding *how*, don't overcomplicate it. At the most fundamental level, your decision is between text, image, audio, and video. We present them to you in increasing level of complexity: image ads are more complex to produce than text ads, audio ads are more complex than image ads, and so on. The increasing level of complexity is a good proxy for an increasing amount of cost to produce. Video ads are typically the most expensive, and text ads are typically the least expensive. As a growth hacker, we recommend that you start with something simple, affordable, and quick to implement, such as text, in order to get an understanding of what works. However, opportunity typically resides where there is complexity. While most of your competitors will run simple text ads, far fewer will invest the time and money into video ads. In summary, start simple and then embrace complexity.

ATTRACTION TACTICS

There is no shortage of ways to attract new prospects. It seems as though there is a new trick or tactic popping up every other day. After looking at how thousands of companies attract customers online, we developed four primary categories to keep Attraction tactics organized: direct, search platforms, branding platforms, and other. By categorizing the infinite amount of Attraction tactics, you can better assess your current weaknesses and prioritize tactics that will address those weaknesses.

Direct: Direct attraction is when someone already knows about you and types your website address directly into her browser. Perhaps that person has done business with you before and recalls your website, or maybe a friend told her about you and she wanted to check out your website. A variety of things can drive direct traffic, ranging from a TV ad to a radio ad. Direct traffic is reflection of overall brand awareness: the more brand awareness, the more direct traffic.

Search Platforms: Attraction from search platforms is when somebody finds you from a search engine. Example search platforms include Google, Bing, and Yahoo. Searches come in three varieties: searches for your brand, searches for a service you provide, and searches for information. There are two ways you can show up when people search: organically or by paid placement. You can improve your organic ranking through search engine optimization (SEO). You can get paid placement through pay-per-click (PPC) advertising. While SEO and PPC tactics come and go, the one thing you can count on is change. New competitors, new rules, regulation updates, and a long list of other factors continually impact your ranking within the search engine algorithms. Therefore, if you want to make search platforms a key part of your Attraction strategy, be prepared to work on a continual basis.

Branding Platforms: Attraction from branding platforms is when somebody finds you on social media or other platforms where your company can be reviewed or talked about. Whether you elect to be part of them or not, branding platforms will pull in information about your business to give consumers a forum to discuss your product or service. Example branding platforms include Facebook, Google+, Twitter, YouTube, Yelp, Houzz, and Angie's List. The common thread is that branding platforms are designed to facilitate conversation around your brand. You can choose to be proactive and control the conversation, or you can be reactive and respond to the conversation. Unfortunately, what you cannot do is ignore branding platforms, because the conversation about your brand will happen with or without your involvement. We advise being proactive on the branding platform that your avatar spends the most time on, as well as the one that is most likely to lead to a buying action. For all other platforms, we recommend being reactive, responding appropriately but not ignoring them.

Other: Attraction from "other" sources is primarily traffic from news sites and partner sites. If you run any online ads outside search, the ads will get served on a variety of news publications and blogs. If you establish any partnerships, hyperlinks back to your site will drive traffic. If you generate any press, the published content will also drive traffic back to your website.

GROWTH HACKTIC

In our experience working with companies that had been featured on ABC's TV show *Shark Tank*, we have learned one surprising PR growth hack. Most companies focus on landing TV appearances, such as getting on *Good Morning America*, but the number of online visitors that offline PR generates is incredibly small. Offline is great for showing a "credibility-lending" logo on your website and a clip on YouTube, but the real money is made with online PR. For example, one *Shark Tank* client has an article that is three years old that is still responsible for 5 percent of all monthly website visitors. What makes online so much easier to land than offline is that the cost to publish can be zero dollars, whereas offline methods have a massive cost structure. If you spoon-feed an online publication unique and original content, the likelihood of getting published is exceptionally high compared to giving the same information to an offline publication.

Whether it's an ad, a backlink, a press mention, or some other method, the "other" Attraction category provides ample opportunities for creative growth hacks that we will talk more about in a growth-hacking exercise later in this chapter.

The intention of having the preceding four categories—direct, search platforms, branding platforms, and other—is to help you parse through the massive volume of Attraction tactics. Take stock of where you are currently getting traffic from online. It's more than likely that one category will be much smaller than the others. Once you have identified the soft spot, you can focus your energy on tactics that will strengthen that category. Prioritizing the activities that will strengthen an Attraction category weakness is a helpful way of identifying your highest return-on-investment (ROI) use of resources.

ADVERTISING ARBITRAGE

One of the frameworks we developed to identify high-ROI Attraction opportunities was the advertising arbitrage framework. The high-level concept is to seek advertising opportunities where advertising inventory supply outpaces advertiser demand. Fundamentally, this will occur when an advertising channel is growing extraordinarily fast (a supply increase), or when an advertising channel is quickly going out of favor (a demand decrease).

As of this writing, an example of a supply-increase advertising arbitrage opportunity is YouTube. More than a billion people visit YouTube every month, it has more reach than any cable network on earth, and the numbers continue to grow at an enormous rate. Most businesses are too lazy or don't have the resources to create video ads, so advertising supply massively outpaces advertiser demand. Given that Google owns YouTube, there is an insane amount of ad targetability, and you can start getting your ad viewed by your ideal buyer for pennies.

A current example of a demand-decrease advertising arbitrage opportunity is the yellow pages. Millions of business owners are pulling out of yellow pages, yet the yellow pages are still used by millions of people. The large yellow pages companies are desperate to sell ad inventory, and because demand is so low, you can pick up massive exposure for pennies on the dollar.

With a bit of research, it will be clear what advertising platforms of relevance to your industry are growing like crazy or quickly falling out of favor. Focus your attention on the extremes. Efficient marketplaces with a predictable supply and demand offer no inherent macroadvantages or arbitrage opportunities.

MARRYING CONTENT WITH COMMERCE

One of the strategies we employ to create incredibly cost-efficient advertising opportunities is to connect content creation with commerce. This concept was pioneered and perfected on the internet by Brian Lee, who founded LegalZoom in 2001. Brian cold-called Bob Shapiro, one of the largest celebrity lawyers at the time, who became famous after successfully defending O. J. Simpson's murder charges. Brian convinced Bob to endorse and join LegalZoom with a cofounder title. This gave LegalZoom immediate credibility and a perennial media machine, because Bob was forever introduced as "Bob Shapiro, defendant of O. J. Simpson and cofounder of LegalZoom." Brian has replicated this strategy multiple times by pairing Kim Kardashian with ShoeDazzle and Jessica Alba with Honest Company.

Another example of someone who successfully arranged the marriage of content and commerce is Ben Lerer, founder of an up-and-coming millennial-dude-focused content site called Thrillist, acquiring Jack Threads, an e-commerce site focused on men. While the acquisition was lambasted by industry pundits at the time, rhetorically asking, "What is a content site doing trying to manage inventory?" the result within a few years was a revenue behemoth of more than one hundred million dollars. While you may not have the national reach to justify partnering with a celebrity or pairing with a global content site, there are ways to scale this strategy down.

Let's say you only have local or regional reach with your

business. There is still an opportunity to merge content creation with commerce. For example, if you run a local roofing company, an endorsement from a local meteorologist could provide significant differentiation from your competitors at a modest price. When executing this strategy, focus on content creators whose audience overlaps with those you are trying to reach. Once you achieve high overlap, approach with a win-win proposition that is more than just a financial transaction. For example, mentioning where and how you intend to promote an endorsement gets folks excited, as that will help them expand their reach and fame (it's "free" advertising for their personal brand).

As it relates to the financial structure of an endorsement, focus on aligning interest and protecting downside. Interest alignment includes things like revenue and equity share and will offset your out-of-pocket expenses. Downside protection is achieved by mitigating upfront costs and commitments. In our experience, it's surprising how affordable endorsements can be at the local and regional level. The local or regional celebrity typically has limited opportunities for expanding income and, if positioned properly, your opportunity is like free money with the mutual benefit of great media exposure.

PERSONALIZATION & QUALIFICATION

As you start to amplify your Attraction, the filtration process of personalizing and qualifying prospects becomes an important way to reduce wasted marketing dollars. Each advertising channel can provide additional insights about your prospect that enables you to tailor your messaging. For example, if you are advertising on the radio, the ad messaging can address "listeners of 99FM," which adds a level of personal touch and helps get more attention from the listeners.

The same personalization principle can be applied to channels both offline and online. The more the message matches the audience, the better your advertising results will be. Intriguingly, qualification can be perceived as personalization, and the end result will be higher-quality prospects. Continuing the radio ad example above, you've probably heard things like, "Listeners of 99FM...if you have a home equity line of credit on your home greater than $50,000 and are currently behind on your payments... then call us now!" Providing listeners with the opportunity to qualify themselves during the Attraction process not only ensures your resources will be better spent but also makes the high-quality prospects feel as if you are talking to them personally.

The lines start to blur when comparing an internet marketer to an online marketer to a digital marketer to a guerilla marketer to a growth hacker, but what differentiates a growth hacker from the rest is the ability to conceive creative, tech-enabled growth strategies when resources are scarce. If etymology and definitions don't pique your interest, skip to the italicized question below. For those that are intrigued by the different marketing titles, here are the distinctions:

MARKETING TITLES

Internet Marketer: Old-school marketers by tech standards. This was a common title back when big businesses were first hearing about the internet.

Online Marketer: Common tech marketing title in the "America Online" days when every business wanted to "get online."

Digital Marketer: Common title for marketers that grew up online and can't imagine life without an internet connection.

Guerilla Marketer: A term coined by Jay Conrad Levinson's book titled *Guerilla Marketing* that was published in 1984. These marketers were accustomed to working creatively with tight budgets but never fully made the transition to the Internet era.

Growth Hacker: A term coined by Sean Ellis in 2010 defined as a tech-savvy and data-driven marketer that understands product and is comfortable working in a resource-constrained environment.

The parameters in the exercise below weed out the internet, online, and digital marketer because they would perform poorly when forced to drive growth without increasing budget. Although the guerilla marketer will propose ideas, the ideas will not have the speed of execution and scale of anything technology related. The growth hacker will devise a creative tech-savvy solution and thrive in the resource-scarce environment.

To help train your mental growth-hacking muscle and, in the process, uncover specific tactics that you can immediately apply to your business, ponder the following question:

Without spending a dollar more on marketing, how can you acquire the most customers in the least time?

At face value, this question seems frustratingly theoretical, but an earnest attempt to address this question produces one specific response: creative thinking.

Let's first address the most debilitating roadblock: starting with zero dollars. As we mentioned previously, there are only two primary resources: money and time. Given that you are starting without the resource of money, you can reduce the scope of potential solutions to those that only consume the resource of time. As a growth hacker, your initial assessment is to look at how your organization is already spending time and identify opportunities where your time spent could benefit someone in a different industry, who then may be inclined to reciprocate. For example, if your sales force is already spending time talking to a customer about your product, is there a complementary product you could offer or refer your leads to? As a specific example, a roofing contractor may start selling his or her roofing leads to a solar company. Conversely, the roofing contractor may offer the solar company a finder's fee for any successful referrals (paying the money out only after collecting money from the referral). Collaboration opportunities exist where your customer base overlaps with a complementary company and is fertile territory for affiliate, joint venture, comarketing, and other similar types of partnership arrangements.

Additionally, are there any opportunities where you

can marry content creation with commerce? In order to structure a deal of this nature without any additional marketing spend, you will have to negotiate an equity or revenue-share arrangement. Or, if you already have a budget for marketing, it may just be a matter of allocating some spend from a different channel. The point is, there are ways to marry content and commerce without spending a dollar more on marketing.

Another way to solve the money problem is through a barter arrangement. With a little creativity, there are a surprising number of opportunities to trade goods or services for exposure and referrals. For example, the way in which Deviate Labs was able to land its first *Shark Tank* client was by waiving the service fee. That was done at no out-of-pocket cost to us; it just took time, and it provided an immense amount of value to the client. The arrangement was premised on the promise that if we provide a lot of value, they would "pay" for our services by introducing us to other *Shark Tank* companies. That arrangement netted us tens of thousands of dollars in business, not to mention a marquee client that differentiated us from our competitors. Done strategically, a barter arrangement where you exchange your product for introductions to other customers can dramatically accelerate the growth of your business.

"

COLLABORATION OPPORTUNITIES
EXIST WHERE YOUR CUSTOMER
BASE OVERLAPS WITH A
COMPLEMENTARY COMPANY AND IS
FERTILE TERRITORY FOR AFFILIATE,
JOINT VENTURE, COMARKETING,
AND OTHER SIMILAR TYPES OF
PARTNERSHIP ARRANGEMENTS.

As your creative collaborations and barter arrangements bear fruit, you unlock resources that can be reinvested back into growth. The act of unlocking more is an important point to underscore, so important that we dubbed this act the "domino theory." The domino theory of growth hacking states that small wins beget progressively larger wins. Your job as a growth hacker is to identify the lead domino, the first tactic to implement, and line up the subsequent dominoes in ascending level of achievability on a path that leads you to your ultimate goal. As an example, one of our clients had a goal of selling fifty thousand dollars of goods through their online marketplace on a monthly basis. When they approached us, they were at zero dollars. The lead domino was to marry content creation and commerce by securing a partnership with a popular national reality TV show that airs on ABC. That deal was secured with primarily an equity-based arrangement, which meant very minimal out of pocket cost.

Once the lead domino had been established, we developed an online competition to identify the best main-street shopping in America. The winning towns would be featured on the TV show and have their shops featured on our client's website. This second domino generated tens of thousands of competition participants and organically generated local press. The local press interest unlocked regional and national press interest as the competition gained momentum.

" "

THE DOMINO THEORY
OF GROWTH HACKING
STATES THAT SMALL WINS BEGET
PROGRESSIVELY LARGER WINS.
YOUR JOB AS A GROWTH HACKER IS
TO IDENTIFY THE LEAD DOMINO, THE
FIRST TACTIC TO IMPLEMENT, AND LINE
UP THE SUBSEQUENT DOMINOES IN
ASCENDING LEVEL OF ACHIEVABILITY
ON A PATH THAT LEADS YOU TO
YOUR ULTIMATE GOAL.

The final domino that we implemented was a redesign of the website. It became a stunningly beautiful shopping experience that featured all the top towns from the competition and included video content of the shops featured on the TV show.

In summary, the TV show partnership unlocked a compelling competition, which unlocked local press, which unlocked regional press, which unlocked national press, which culminated in a TV show that led to a redesign of the website that included video content from the show and featured the top towns from the competition, which led to the achievement of the ultimate goal. Had we gone straight for national TV exposure, we would have paid tens of thousands for a commercial and more than likely received no incremental lift in sales. Instead we got creative, started small, and progressively pushed over more dominoes until we achieved the seemingly impossible on a zero-dollar advertising budget.

GROWTH HACKING APPLIED

It shocked us when exposure to seven million American households resulted in less than a hundred sales.

Our client wholeheartedly believed his product should be in every household in America. The Sharks, on the other hand, were not convinced. In fact, Mr. Wonderful literally called the product a "piece of crap."

As for us, we let the data speak for itself.

Despite Mr. Wonderful criticizing the product, there were still some people that purchased. These were the true fans and became the basis for our avatar.

Once we had a clearly defined avatar, we studied the ideal buyers' every online behavior. We sought answers for a variety of questions such as "What did they search for?" "What websites did they frequent?" and "What forums did they contribute to?"

Ultimately, we focused the marketing efforts on the search platform. We isolated searches with clear purchase intent to provide the client with an immediate payback cycle. We steered away from branding platforms as the payback cycle can take much longer and our client was days away from financial insolvency. Fortunately, with the right attraction in place, our client was able to avert disaster and keep the business afloat.

In spite of the Sharks swimming away from the investment opportunity, the company has grown into a massively profitable business and landed big-box retail partnerships, all without having to give up an ounce of ownership to the greedy bite of a Shark.

ATTRACTION TAKEAWAYS

- While the initial out-of-pocket expense may be low, advertising inventory scalable, and ad serving automatable for online attraction, there is a certain time when an adept growth hacker should pursue offline opportunities.

- The growth hack used by Silicon Valley tech companies to parse through the multitude of digital demographic data is to create an avatar, a digital representation of your ideal buyer.

- When marketing to your avatar, focus first on when the avatar is in a buying mood or likely to take a buying action, where your avatar spends time, and how best to reach the avatar (text, image, audio, or video).

- The four primary categories to keep Attraction tactics organized are direct, search platforms, branding platforms, and other.

- A framework for identifying high-ROI Attraction opportunities is called advertising arbitrage: seek advertising opportunities where advertising inventory supply outpaces advertiser demand.
- A strategy for creating cost-efficient advertising opportunities is to marry content creation with commerce.
- As you start to amplify your Attraction, the filtration process of personalizing and qualifying prospects enables you to reduce wasted marketing dollars.
- The domino theory of growth hacking states that small wins beget progressively larger wins. Identify the lead domino, the first tactic to implement, and line up the subsequent dominoes in ascending level of achievability on a path that leads you to your ultimate goal.
- Collaboration opportunities exist where your customer base overlaps with a complementary company and is fertile territory for affiliate, joint venture, comarketing, and other similar types of partnership arrangements.

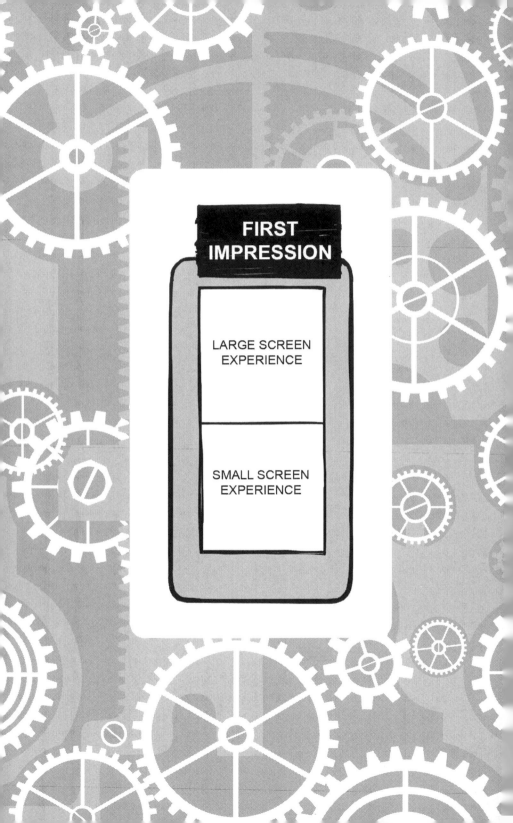

FIRST IMPRESSION

Set a powerful first impression, giving your prospects a consistent, personalized, and professional experience.

Growth can be difficult. Like a teenager entering adulthood, there's bound to be awkward transitions, identity crises, and growing pains. No one knows the trialing "teenage" phase of business better than a real estate developer client of ours based on the luxurious Caribbean island of St. Barts. He aspired to become a Caribbean real estate mogul, but felt stuck branded as a middle-market, mainstream realtor.

St. Barts is home away from home for A-list celebrities such as Beyonce, Jay-Z, and Jon Bon Jovi. Although the island coastline is dotted with hundreds of megamansion vacation homes, our soon-to-be client was stuck selling condos and small homes the size of the maid's quarters. He desperately wanted to grow up and play in the big leagues.

In an effort to attract wealthy clientele, he purchased TV ads at all the island's five-star hotels. In addition to buying up the TV spots, he spent a huge amount of time and effort creating a commercial. He justified the investment by reasoning that well-to-do individuals staying at a high-end hotel would fall in love with the island, decide to buy a vacation home there, see his ad, and call him.

The TV ads fell flat on their faces.

He didn't land a single megamansion client. Could it be that his ads were poorly created, thereby failing to attract the ultrawealthy? That's unlikely, considering that he hired a reputable company to produce the ads. Perhaps he was a victim of poor timing and the St. Barts real estate market was in a slump? This couldn't have been the case, because his competitors were doing just fine.

Despite the setback, our client remained tenacious. Determined to penetrate the megamansion market, he reached out to us and asked for help. Was the problem Attraction? Or was growth actually inhibited by his fledgling First Impression?

THE EVOLUTION OF THE FIRST IMPRESSION

The first impression, by definition, is established when someone first comes in contact with your brand or business. Pre-internet, the first impression was established when someone walked into your store or office. One could quickly ascertain what products you offered, whether you were a big business or a small one, and whether you were organized or messy, and they could draw dozens of other conclusions. The investment required to improve your first impression was quite costly. For example, if you want to appear like a big business, you were going to need a big office with lots of employees, and that could quickly cost hundreds of thousands of dollars.

Online, your storefront or office is your website. Visitors draw conclusions based on a million little things, such as whether your website loads quickly, how polished your web design appears, and whether you own a .com domain. Rather than you as an individual investing hundreds of thousands of dollars to polish your first impression as you would in the offline world, the internet levels the playing field and you can "look big and professional" for a fraction of that amount. Despite technology leveling the playing field, it also changes incredibly rapidly. A storefront or office that is a few years old can still appear "just like new," but a website that is a few years old can look archaic.

In the present tech-enabled economy, the one constant is change. The physical storefront changed marginally since the Industrial Revolution in the mid-1800s. Ironically, stores that didn't change over long periods of time are often looked upon with fond feelings of nostalgia. Online, an old website doesn't conjure the same feelings of nostalgia. Instead, an old website is often met with fear and frustration, as dated websites often have privacy breaches and lack device compatibility. The point of first impression has evolved rapidly since the introduction of technology, as follows:

FIRST IMPRESSION EVOLUTION

- Storefront or Office (twentieth century)
- Desktop Website (mainstream circa 2000)
- Social Media Presence (mainstream circa 2005)
- Mobile-Friendly Website (mainstream circa 2008)
- Future: Virtual + Augmented-Reality Presence (mainstream circa 2020?)

The challenge is that the evolution of the first impression makes cumulative additions. You can't just focus on having a polished mobile-friendly website; you also need a professional social media presence, a solid desktop version of your website, and, in many cases, a nice storefront or office. The compounding effect of these changes forces you to make certain trade-off decisions when deciding how to best allocate your resources. In the subsequent sections, we will explore some frameworks for how to maximize the return on First Impression investment.

WHEN CHANGE IS GOOD

It's easy for marketing pundits, gurus, and ninjas to stand on top of their soapbox and proclaim, "Everything you know about marketing has changed; if you aren't advertising on social media, you're dead," or "Mobilegeddon is here; you need a mobile website yesterday," or "Virtual reality will totally change everything; you need to be prepared with a 3D website." Sweeping statements of doomsday hyperbole make headlines, and the headlines make you feel that if you aren't the first company in your area or industry to adapt, you are going to be disrupted and destroyed.

In Silicon Valley, there is a mantra, "change is good," that gets misinterpreted, misused, and mistaken as gospel. The mantra is an oversimplification that overlooks the cost-benefit analysis required to determine *when* change is good.

As the saying goes, the trouble with being a pioneer is that you're the one who takes the arrows. Is it better to be a first mover and risk getting pelted with an arrow or a fast follower and follow the body shields in front of you?

FIRST MOVE OR FAST FOLLOW?

Although this section is intended to address your first impression as it pertains to marketing, the concepts in this section can be applied in any situation where technology and innovation impact your business. When it comes to the preservation of resources, a fast-follow strategy is consistently superior to a first-mover strategy, particularly pertaining to your first impression. The trick is to figure out whom to follow.

The early adopter inevitably pays a premium. As processes get perfected, technology gets streamlined, and more providers compete for your business, costs are driven down. For example, the cost of a website in the 1990s was millions of dollars, it took many months to build, and it had to be built from scratch. In less than a decade, you could produce a better quality website for a few thousand dollars using a template over a weekend.

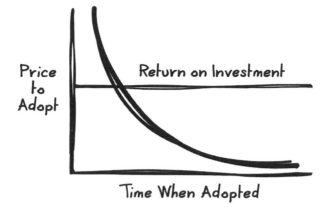

Price to Adopt

Return on Investment

Time When Adopted

PRICE OF ADOPTION CURVE

Your task is to assess your potential return on investment realized when the technology is implemented and adopt when the benefits outweigh the cost. Depending on the potential return on investment, first movers often find themselves wasting money on expensive technology. As a general rule, a fast-follow technology adoption strategy mitigates the risk of losing money while maximizing the duration of enjoying a return on investment.

That being said, at first glance it may appear that the late adopter will reap the largest return because the difference between price to adopt and return on investment will be maximized. However, there is a tangible opportunity cost that grows larger as time passes after the intersection between cost and return. Continuing with the website

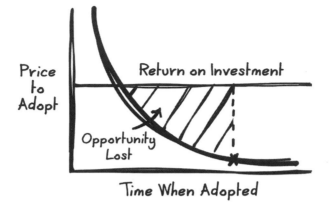

example, the early adopters that spent millions of dollars weren't local businesses; they were multinational brands like Coca-Cola. If Coca-Cola had waited ten years before they adopted, they would have lost billions of dollars in market share to early-adopting competitors such as Pepsi-Cola and nimble new entrants such as Richard Branson's Virgin Cola that made use of early web-marketing tactics.

Lack of innovation becomes a growing liability. In the technology hotbed of Silicon Valley, the accrued liability caused by delaying innovation has its own term: "technical debt." As all businesses are becoming more and more technology dependent, managing and mitigating accrued technical debt is now a necessary practice that businesses outside Silicon Valley completely overlook.

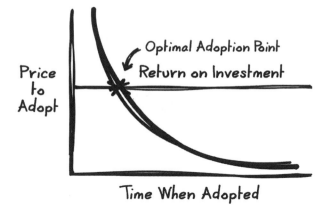

Price to Adopt

Optimal Adoption Point

Return on Investment

Time When Adopted

Although the pundits aren't incorrect when they proclaim things like, "Virtual reality will totally change everything; you need to be prepared with a 3D website," you need to apply the price of adoption framework in order to determine when to adopt. Coca-Cola can justify spending millions of dollars to build a 3D website years before the average business. However, you can be assured that the adoption cost will drop dramatically over time, and you can look to other similar industries to determine what type of return on investment you can expect and when to "fast follow." By applying the price of adoption framework, you can visually see that the optimal adoption point is as close to the intersection of the Adoption Cost curve and the Return on Investment line.

The distinction between first mover and fast follower is highly relative. You could be the first company in the world, or the first company in your industry, or the first company in your geography, or some other relative qualifier. While Silicon Valley gives the perception that first is best, one of the many secrets is that established companies wait to see how the first movers play out and then adopt when there is a clear return on investment. For companies outside the Valley, keeping an eye on companies outside your industry enables you to observe what works and apply that to your industry. You reap the benefits of being the first mover in your niche, with the cost savings of being a fast follower relative to companies outside your industry.

COPYCAT

The "wait-and-see" approach that established tech companies in Silicon Valley take as referenced above is typically followed by the "copycat" tactic.

We're conditioned to believe that copycats are bad, and there are obvious instances where there are potential copyright infringements, but as it pertains to polishing your first impression, it's an incredibly cost-effective growth hack.

For example, as mobile technology emerged, there was a period of time when everyone knew they needed to redesign their website in order to have a polished first impression for individuals coming in on their phone. The early adopters

> WHEN IT COMES TO THE PRESERVATION OF RESOURCES, A FAST-FOLLOW STRATEGY IS CONSISTENTLY SUPERIOR TO A FIRST-MOVER STRATEGY, PARTICULARLY PERTAINING TO YOUR FIRST IMPRESSION. THE TRICK IS TO FIGURE OUT WHOM TO FOLLOW.

spent tons of money creating new mobile-friendly sites from scratch. Rather than adopting early, the savvy growth hacker would wait until the early adopters had implemented their new First Impression technology and quickly copycat the best one and marginally tweak it for their use. It's far cheaper to stand on the proverbial shoulders of early-adopting giants than reinvent the proverbial wheel.

GROWTH HACKING APPLIED

The aspiring St. Barts real estate mogul had a clear vision of his end goal, but after the TV ads fell flat, he looked to us to help him achieve mogul status.

During our diligence we observed something surprising. Although our client had written the TV ads off as a failure, they were actually a quiet success. When we looked at the website data, we saw a clear spike in visitors after the ads went live. The ads were attracting prospects just fine; it was the First Impression that was falling flat.

The ultra-wealthy vacationers came to St. Barts to escape the hustle and grind of their work, and they weren't about to let a real estate transaction tarnish their rest and relaxation. However, the moment the wealthy vacationers got back home from their vacation, they would jump online, and the first destination they visited was the website they saw referenced on TV. Our client, expecting he was going

> **IT'S FAR CHEAPER TO STAND ON THE PROVERBIAL SHOULDERS OF EARLY-ADOPTING GIANTS THAN REINVENT THE PROVERBIAL WHEEL.**

to get direct phone calls from the TV ad, not web traffic, had neglected to fix his First Impression that hadn't been touched for years and wasn't even mobile-friendly. The dilapidated First Impression stopped the wealthy prospects in their tracks and prompted them to look elsewhere.

The technology implemented in the St. Barts real estate market lags the competitive early-adopting US real estate market by several years. In order to cost-consciously improve our client's digital First Impression, we compiled a list of websites from the top American real estate professionals that the ultra-wealthy trusted with their business. After a conversation with our client, we swiped the best elements from the top sites and created a beautiful, brand-new First Impression. The result was a First Impression that was ten-times better than any of his St. Barts real estate competitors and was an order of magnitude cheaper to build than the early-adopting American real estate professionals.

After a First Impression facelift, ultra-wealthy leads started pouring in. Our client went from listing $500,000 condos to $5,500,000 beachside estates literally overnight. The return on this First Impression investment exceeded our client's most optimistic expectations.

While not every First Impression transformation story is as extreme, even a marginal improvement can pay significant dividends over time. For some companies, dividends come in the form of online sales, but many companies benefit in more intangible ways, such as winning competitive requests for proposals (RFPs), attracting higher-quality employee talent, and landing industry partnerships. The benefits may not be directly attributable, but that is not to say a polished first impression doesn't play a key role. Prospects judge a book by its cover; make sure your cover entices them to open your book and read your story.

FIRST IMPRESSION TAKEAWAYS

- Despite technology leveling the playing field, it also changes rapidly, and you can quickly appear dated or become obsolete in a fraction of the time it takes a physical storefront or office to become obsolete.
- A fast-follow technology adoption strategy mitigates the risk of losing money while maximizing the duration of enjoying a return on investment.
- Look outside your industry for best practices to follow so you can still benefit from first-mover advantage in your niche.
- It's better to stand on the proverbial shoulders of giants than reinvent the proverbial wheel; the copycat tactic will save you thousands.
- The benefits of having a polished first impression may not be 100 percent attributable to sales growth, but that is not to say it doesn't play a key role.

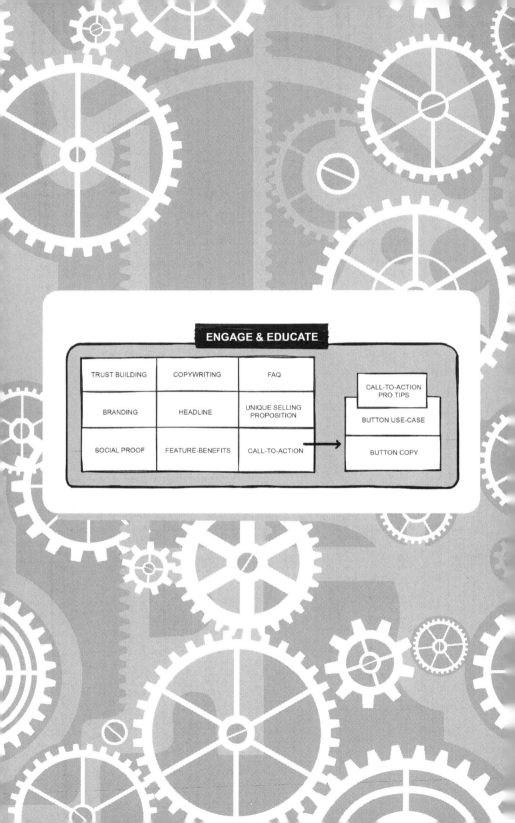

ENGAGE & EDUCATE

TRUST BUILDING	COPYWRITING	FAQ
BRANDING	HEADLINE	UNIQUE SELLING PROPOSITION
SOCIAL PROOF	FEATURE-BENEFITS	CALL-TO-ACTION

CALL-TO-ACTION PRO TIPS
BUTTON USE-CASE
BUTTON COPY

ENGAGE & EDUCATE

Engage and patiently educate your prospects so they have all the information they need to comfortably buy from you.

They were touted as one of Mark Cuban's and Robert Herjavec's most successful *Shark Tank* investments. When their episode aired on ABC, the company completely sold out of product. When the Sharks introduced them to big-box retailers such as Walmart and Target, they immediately inked huge wholesale orders. But behind closed doors, the owners were suffering.

While the Shark's big-box retail connections were helpful, as a small start-up the company didn't have the economies of scale to drive down manufacturing costs. The heavy-weight retailers gave the company take-it-or-leave-it terms that left the small start-up with razor-thin profit margins. But they had to accept; otherwise, they would appear ungrateful for the Shark's introductions and risk spoiling future introduction opportunities.

Despite having gone from less than one hundred thousand dollars to more than one million dollars in annual revenue overnight, the company's profit was virtually nonexistent, and the owners were struggling to pay the bills at home.

Not wanting to disappoint or worry their *Shark Tank* investors, the company only smiled and nodded when Mark and Robert excitedly congratulated them on their "hockey stick" revenue growth. When ABC announced an extension show, *Beyond the Tank*, to feature *Shark Tank* success stories, the company was immediately slated to be one of the first episodes filmed.

The company was scheduled to film in three months. They desperately needed to make a profit so they could pay their bills at home and show everyone that they were living the American Dream. Using the last money left over from their *Shark Tank* investment, they engaged us to grow high-margin direct-to-consumer sales via their website. If we didn't immediately hack growth, the company risked embarrassing themselves, Mark, and Robert as the *Shark Tank* success story that was actually a failure.

When we assessed the business using the ASP™ framework, their Attraction was solid, their First Impression was sufficient, but their Engage & Educate component was worrisome. Given the time constraint, we didn't have the luxury of methodically hypothesizing, testing, and iterating; we absolutely had to get this right the first time. We focused the last remaining resources on a complete overhaul of their Engage & Educate component.

The ASP™ framework was now being scrutinized by Mark Cuban and Robert Herjavec and soon-to-be millions of *Shark Tank* fans. Would the ASP™ withstand the scrutiny and save the company from complete embarrassment?

ANCIENT MODES OF PERSUASION

Before we dive into the nine modern modalities of Engage & Educate, you must first understand the three ancient modes of persuasion that were famously first introduced by Aristotle more than 2,400 years ago. Though we may have fancier communication tools, such as computers and cell phones, than our Aristotelian predecessors, human psychology has changed very little. Stripped of our fancy tools, there are only three fundamental ways to persuade. The three "rhetorical appeals," as Aristotle called them, are as follows:

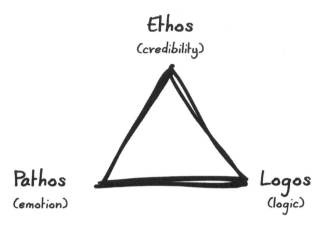

Appeals to ethos are persuasive tactics that build your credibility—for example, a marquee client or an impressive press mention. Appeals to pathos are persuasive tactics that appeal to your audience's emotion—for example, a stunning photo or a captivating client testimonial. Appeals to logos are persuasive tactics that are supported by logic—for example, facts and figures, and features and benefits.

In order to maximize the persuasive effect of your communication, you must make all three rhetorical appeals: ethos, pathos, and logos. Most businesses aimlessly communicate with no purpose or intention, hoping that eventually they will say something that resonates and results in a purchase. A growth hacker uses crystal-clear communi-

"

IN ORDER TO MAXIMIZE THE PERSUASIVE EFFECT OF YOUR COMMUNICATION, YOU MUST MAKE ALL THREE RHETORICAL APPEALS: ETHOS, PATHOS, AND LOGOS.

cation that is strategically designed to engage, educate, and ultimately sell. When all components of Engage & Educate are implemented, the persuasive effects will be so powerful that your growth rate will seem propelled by a magical force.

The heart and soul of your communication is rooted in Aristotle's rhetorical framework. However, there are so many modern tools and tactics that it can be challenging to know how and where to implement ethos, pathos, and logos. So we created the nine modern modalities of persuasion to help you clearly see how and where to implement Aristotle's rhetorical framework in the present day.

NINE MODERN MODALITIES OF PERSUASION

There are subtle psychological queues that influence visitors to take a specific action. In the offline world, a casino serves as a good case study to illustrate the many ways one can subconsciously influence human behavior. From the windowless casino floors where a circadian sense of time is completely lost, to the free alcohol that lowers gambling inhibitions, to the intentionally loud coin-clanking of slot-machine payouts so that all one hears is the exhilarating sound of winning, casinos are multibillion-dollar money machines psychologically fine-tuned to take your money and make you feel good while it happens.

In the online world, your website is your metaphorical casino, and there are an equal number of psychological tactics that can "stack the cards" in your favor. The nine modalities of Engage & Educate are as follows:

NINE MODERN MODALITIES OF ENGAGE & EDUCATE

1. Trust Building
2. Branding
3. Unique Selling Proposition
4. Headline
5. Feature-Benefits
6. Copywriting
7. Social Proof
8. Frequently Asked Questions (FAQs)
9. Call-to-Action

1. TRUST BUILDING (ETHOS / PATHOS)

Before someone starts reading and engaging with your content, there is a three-second period of suspense where the aesthetics (*ethos*) and general feeling (*pathos*) of your site signal to your visitor whether or not to continue on. Passing the "three-second test" is a reflection of your ability to subconsciously convey that you are someone that can be trusted to provide what the visitor is looking for. Some elements that affect your ability to gain the trust of your avatar in the first three seconds include the layout and design of your website, the style of writing you use, the images you choose to portray, and the other eight components enumerated below.

A few user tests or an examination of the bounce rate (the percentage of people that leave your site versus continue on to another page) and overall time spent on your site will give you a general sense for whether you are passing the three-second test. If you don't want to overcomplicate your assessment, ask yourself, "Do I feel proud to send people to my website?" For many, the answer is no. At that point, your website is more of a liability than an asset, and an update is in order.

2. BRANDING (ETHOS)

While branding is grossly misunderstood and often overemphasized for businesses that are not among the Fortune 500, there are a few brand basics that every business needs to apply. The question is less about whether your brand is "good" or "bad"; that is too ambiguous and subjective. The question is whether your brand is consistent or inconsistent. The consistent application of the following brand basics will put you ahead of the vast majority of your competitors:

BRAND BASICS

- **Logo:** vertical + horizontal + color + black on white + white on black + iconized
- **Colors:** a three- or five-color spectrum
- **Typography:** headline fonts as well as a reading-style font
- **Voice:** a set of rules for writing produced by the brand

As great as jingles, slogans, and brand values are, they don't move the needle for small- and medium-sized businesses. As long as you establish the basics, and you use them consistently, you will be fine. The value of having a brand is that people will know it's you before you tell them it's you. For example, if someone sees your ad and then comes to your website, and the website has the same style as the ad, then he will immediately know he is in the right place. People subconsciously trust and ascribe credibility (*ethos*) to that which is predictable.

3. UNIQUE SELLING PROPOSITION (PATHOS / LOGOS)

Your unique selling proposition (USP), also referred to as your "unique selling point" and synonymous with your "unique value proposition" (UVP), is a succinct summation of how your company is different from your competitors.

Let's looks at the shoe industry, a highly commoditized and competitive industry, for three examples of USPs:

- Toms: For every pair of shoes you buy, they donate a pair to someone in need.
- Zappos: Every shoe purchase has free returns and is backed by best-in-class customer service.
- Jimmy Choo: A status symbol putting you in the same shoes worn on Hollywood's red carpet.

Many companies are wary of advertising points of differentiation for fear of alienating an audience and missing out on a potential sale. However, in an attempt to be all things to all people, you end up being nothing to everybody. A clear and effective USP will convey credibility (*ethos*) and subconsciously tap into the emotional desire of your avatar (*pathos*).

4. HEADLINE (LOGOS)

A headline should immediately draw attention and be the very first words that people read when visiting your website. In its purest form, it needs to immediately signal to your visitor that she landed in the right spot. It's easy to get cute and try and say something clever; but "cute" and "clever" quickly degenerate to "convoluted" and "confusing." Instead, aim for a headline that provides instant clarity (*logos*). Here are a couple formulas for crafting instant-clarity headlines:

INSTANT-CLARITY HEADLINE FORMULAS

[What You Do] + [What Makes You Unique] + [Geographic Reach]

Example: Residential & Commercial Roofing Since 1929 Serving Los Angeles and Surrounding Area

[End Result the Customer Wants] + [Specific Period of Time] + [Address the Objections]

Example: Hot Fresh Pizza Delivered to Your Door in Thirty Minutes or It's Free

Some have asked, "Why don't I see Apple ads that look like that?" The answer is two-fold: one, Apple is a massive company with tons of products and services, and when they're buying a billboard or TV spot that's hitting millions of eyeballs, it's a better long-run ROI to sell the brand with a tagline than sell a singular product with a headline; two, they do use headlines like the above, but they typically save them for more targeted advertising. To distinguish the difference between a tagline, a slogan, and a headline, here are examples from the iPad Air campaign:

TAGLINE VS. SLOGAN VS. HEADLINE

Tagline

"Think Different"

Slogan

"Change is in the Air"

Headline

"Our Most Advanced Technology in a Magical and Revolutionary Device at an Unbelievable Price"

While the lines of distinction are often blurred, as a general rule a tagline represents the company, a slogan represents a product or service, and a headline sells the product or service to a specific audience. If you are a large company doing national and international brand-awareness ad campaigns, then developing a tagline and slogan will be worth your time and attention. However, if you are a small- or medium-sized business, you are typically selling your product or service to a specific audience, so you don't need to fret about taglines and slogans.

5. FEATURE-BENEFITS (PATHOS / LOGOS)

To support the content conveyed in the headline and

"

...IN AN ATTEMPT
TO BE ALL THINGS TO
ALL PEOPLE, YOU END
UP BEING NOTHING
TO EVERYBODY.

appeal to those that respond to logic, the crafting of clear "feature-benefits" is a core characteristic of the Engage & Educate component of the ASP™. What is important to emphasize is that this component is not features AND benefits, but rather a merged mash-up that marries the two together.

FEATURE-BENEFITS

[What Something Is] + [What Something Does]

Example (Apple's iPod): 1GB of MP3s that puts 1,000s of Songs in Your Pocket

While there is no set rule, feature-benefits often come in sets of three or more and are typically formatted as digestible snippets. Given the gravity of importance associated with feature-benefits, it often is helpful to attach a visual icon to complement each snippet of feature-benefit text. To complement the example above, one may add an MP3 icon so that individuals skimming the content (which is the majority of individuals) will be drawn in with the visual icon hook to consume the feature-benefit text.

Most individuals struggle tying features to tangible,

emotion-inducing benefits. A simple trick to determine whether you've crafted a compelling feature-benefit is the "So what?" test. After every feature ask the question, "So what?" If the question is unanswered, you are missing the benefit. For example, had Apple's iPod ad simply said "1GB of MP3s," and you asked, "So what?" the feature-benefit would clearly feel incomplete. After all, "1GB of MP3s" means nothing without the follow-up statement: "that puts 1,000s of songs in your pocket." Consumers can relate "1,000s of songs in your pocket" with happiness (listening to music) (*pathos*) and convenience (all within your pocket) (*logos*).

6. COPYWRITING (PATHOS)

Copywriting is the art and skill of writing in a manner that persuades and seduces your reader toward an action, viewpoint, opinion, or sale. A person that is an excellent writer may not necessarily be an excellent copywriter. An excellent copywriter requires an intimate understanding of the reader, your avatar. By understanding your avatar's wants, needs, and desires, you can connect with her pain and pleasure points. It's less about appealing to your avatar on an intellectual level with technical jargon and more about appealing to your avatar on an emotional level (*pathos*). Write as if you were talking to a close friend.

Once you have a sense for the types of words, phrases, questions, and comments your customers have, your next step is to adopt a writing prose that feels direct and personal. When writing customer-centric copy, avoid "we," "my," "us," and "our"; instead, use "you" and "your." Imagine talking to a single prospective customer about your business; that is the conversational tone and direct feeling you want to convey when engaging and educating people about your company.

7. SOCIAL PROOF (ETHOS)

After you've passed the three-second test as discussed in the Trust Building component previously, layering on additional elements of social proof will solidify your trust and maximize your influence. Social proof, referred to as "informational social influence" among psychologists,

"

WHEN WRITING CUSTOMER-
CENTRIC COPY, AVOID "WE,"
"MY," "US," AND "OUR"; INSTEAD,
USE "YOU" AND "YOUR."

states that we mimic the actions of others when we are unsure what to do. We are psychologically hardwired to conform to the actions of our "tribe" as a shortcut survival mechanism. The reason a toddler is going to want the exact same toy as their playmate, despite there being dozens of other perfectly good toys laying around, is that the toddler wants the one that is credibly proven (*ethos*) to lead to the greatest satisfaction.

Here are some examples of social proof:

- Endorsements (experts, celebrities)
- Client mentions (logos, testimonials)
- Partner mentions (logos, quotes)
- Press mentions (logos, quotes)
- Reviews
- Ratings
- Awards
- Social media following / connections / likes / shares
- Number of people served

The more uncertainty, the more conformity. In other words, the more competitive your market is, the more influence social proof will have. Then, the more social proof you have, the more influence you will have. The multiple-source effect is that when multiple different sources are cited, each individual source is perceived as having more influence.

A study was done comparing the influence of five reviews done in one voice to five different voices, and although the content was identical, the perceived influence of the different voices had a dramatically greater influence. Although it may feel repetitive to you, a diverse array of social proof will multiply the effect of your influence.

8. FREQUENTLY ASKED QUESTIONS (FAQS) (PATHOS / LOGOS)

The manifestation of the ASP™ is a digital representation of your top salesperson. One of the key differentiators between a good salesperson and a great salesperson is the ability to gracefully handle client objections. Frequently asked questions (FAQs) are your digital opportunity to handle objections, and you can do so in a way that captures your salesperson's most eloquent rebuttal. It may appear counterintuitive to prompt questions that may not even be on the mind of your prospective customers, but the questions can be framed in a way that positions the product or service in a favorable light. For example, as opposed to saying, "Does your window-cleaning service kill birds?" you can frame the question as "How does Mr. Clean Window Company help birds steer clear from my sparkling clean windows?" As with any great salesman, you can transform even the most jarring objections into a positive FAQ through a blend of logic (*logos*) and emotion (*pathos*).

FAQs can also be used to boost search-engine position-ing and decrease the cost of purchased traffic. Without going down the rabbit hole of search-engine algorithms and pay-per-click cost calculations, you can see that the more relevant text your page has, the better. Structurally, we advise tucking your FAQs toward the bottom of the page, followed by a repeat of the primary call-to-action. The next section will give you more clarity around what we mean by "primary call-to-action."

9. CALL-TO-ACTION (PATHOS)

The term "call-to-action" is a hyphenated way of saying, "Tell people what to do next." While you want to give prospects a breadth of options, you can subtly shepherd visitors to take a preferred action. As such, it's important for you to identify the primary, secondary, tertiary, and so on calls-to-action prioritized based on what fits best with your operation and industry. Here are some examples of different calls-to-action:

- Book an appointment online
- Call our 1-800 number
- Click here to buy
- Request a proposal
- Submit a contact form
- Instant-message us

"

FREQUENTLY ASKED QUESTIONS (FAQS) ARE YOUR DIGITAL OPPORTUNITY TO HANDLE OBJECTIONS...

The quantity of calls-to-action often depends on the size of your operations and nature of your business. A small- or medium-sized business might only have a primary and secondary call-to-action. There are diminished returns and additional operational costs the more options you present to your prospects.

Once you have prioritized your preferred calls-to-action, there are several tactics for influencing behavior so that people take action without even thinking about it (*pathos*). The primary call-to-action should be visible "above the fold" (the section of the webpage before you start scrolling down). Some individuals already know that they want to purchase from you when they arrive on your page, it's your job to give them a way to take immediate action. Putting the primary call-to-action in a button will add the visual queue that indicates "what to do next."

"

**PUTTING
THE PRIMARY
CALL-TO-ACTION IN A
BUTTON WILL ADD THE
VISUAL QUEUE THAT
INDICATES "WHAT
TO DO NEXT."**

GROWTH HACKTIC

Button Copy

- Lead with a familiar verb (e.g., Get, Grab, Download, Start, Apply).
- Be specific (avoid only using a generic phrase like "Click Here").
- Be clear about what happens next (you can add copy below the button to add clarity; e.g., "Step 1 of 3").
- Don't be afraid of long button text; adding pronouns (e.g., "my"), articles (e.g., "the"), and prepositions (e.g., "for") can make you sound more human and friendly.
- Add a benefit. If there is clear benefit that occurs when an action is taken, make that known (e.g., "Protect My Computer").

Button Design

- Contrast the color so it's different than the other colors on the page (don't worry, there is no "magic" color; just make it different).
- Make it "feel" clickable (add mouse hover effects so users are subconsciously swayed to want to click).

On pages with larger amounts of content where you have to do some scrolling, it's best practice to repeat the key call-to-action at the bottom of the page.

The calls-to-action that are not primary can be situated around the periphery of the page to de-emphasize the likelihood of the visitor choosing a less preferred action. Whether that is a slide-out sidebar tab or a phone number in the upper right-hand corner, the secondary and tertiary calls-to-action can be placed in less conspicuous locations and don't necessarily need to be put inside a button. In conclusion, as long as you make it clear "what to do next," you will be fine.

GREATER THAN THE SUM OF ITS PARTS

The nine modalities, in isolation, are not enough to substantially engage and educate a prospect to a point where she feels comfortable taking action. For example, you can have endless amount of social proof, but without a clear call-to-action, it's all purposeless puffery. However, when you begin to group the components together, the collective value increases exponentially.

The question we are often asked is, "Do I need every component on every page?" And the answer depends. The homepage, landing pages (specific webpages that you send targeted traffic to), and, to some extent, product pages benefit from maximizing the engagement and educational value. Other pages, such as news articles, about us, and contact us, will not need every component to be effective.

Prioritize your effectiveness improvement based on traffic. Start with your high-traffic homepage, and work your way outward to pages that get incrementally less traffic.

The follow-up question we are often asked is, "How do I know if what I'm doing is working?" The simple answer is, "Track and measure." The complex answer includes a discussion of analytics tools, but the tools change so rapidly that they're likely to be obsolete by the time you read this. The principle that is worth applying is that the best analytics tool is the one you actually use. At present, Google Analytics is free, powerful, and a staple tool for most websites. As you improve the Engage & Educate component of your ASP™, you will typically see average time spent on your site increase, bounce rate decrease, average pages viewed per visitor increase, and, if it all comes together correctly, conversion rate (ability to convert a visitor into a prospect and a paying customer) increase. Analytics can get very complicated, so if you only have time to track one number, track the conversion rate.

GROWTH HACKING APPLIED

It was all hands on deck as the *Shark Tank* client mentioned at the beginning of this chapter was scheduled to film their *Beyond the Tank* episode in just three months. The company founders were petrified that the episode

66

...THE BEST ANALYTICS
TOOL IS THE ONE YOU
ACTUALLY USE.

would reveal the truth, that their profits were barely covering living expenses.

The *Shark Tank* exposure and subsequent investment from Mark Cuban and Robert Herjavec led to massive amounts of press, which created one of the strongest Attraction components we had seen for a company at that stage. However, when we combed through the data, we saw that the company's conversion rate from visitors to purchases was only half of that of their industry peers. When you extrapolate a 50 percent conversion rate reduction across tens of thousands of monthly visitors, the result is a painfully large amount of missed revenue. The company's Engage & Educate component was virtually nonexistent, and in order to drive high-margin direct-to-consumer sales, we needed to completely overhaul their website.

We immediately went to work on integrating the Engage & Educate subcomponents, focusing heavily on the high-traffic homepage. We transformed their homepage from a small splash page to a lengthy hybrid sales page that served a variety of audiences. The above-the-fold space at the top was dedicated to a lifestyle image with the products used in context and an emphasis on the call-to-action: going to the shop. The high-fidelity image immediately passed the three-second trust-building test and conveyed credibility (*ethos*) and appealed to emotion (*pathos*). Additionally, we added the company slogan in the above-the-fold space, which served the dual purpose of building the brand and presenting the unique selling proposition (USP).

Further down the homepage, we embedded press mentions and testimonials that provided social proof and further solidified the appeal to ethos. Injected within the body content of the page were secondary calls-to-action. They were clearly copywritten statements put inside a red button that contrasted starkly against the white background. The product blurbs contained customer-centric copy that used phrases pulled directly from customer reviews on Amazon.

The page concluded with a direct appeal to logic (logos) with a visual and text-based reference to the various credibility components (e.g., certifications) of the products. An appeal to logic was intentionally placed lower on the page because visitors that make emotion-based decisions were more likely to click through much earlier, whereas visitors that make logic-based decisions were more likely to scroll through the whole page. The page finished with a repeat of the key call-to-action, go to the shop, so that the next step is perfectly clear.

By revamping the Engage & Educate component and ensuring all nine subcomponents were tightly integrated, we doubled our client's conversion rate, the most important number to track when assessing the Engage & Educate component performance, putting it in alignment with other top-performing e-commerce sites. The founders were ecstatic as the increase in conversion rate doubled their profitability accordingly and they were able to pay off their mounting bills at home. Ultimately, the company lived up to the tremendous success-story expectations when they filmed their wildly popular *Beyond the Tank* episode.

ENGAGE & EDUCATE TAKEAWAYS

- Aristotle's *Rhetoric* outlines the ancient modes of persuasion: ethos (credibility), pathos (emotion), logos (logic). In order to maximize the persuasive effect of your communication, you must make all three rhetorical appeals.
- Passing the three-second test is a reflection of your ability to subconsciously convey that you are someone that can be trusted to provide what the visitor is looking for.
- The value of having a brand is that people will know it's you before you tell them it's you.

- Your unique selling proposition (USP) is a succinct summation of how your company is different from your competitors.
- A tagline represents the company, a slogan represents a product or service, and a headline sells the product or service to a specific audience.
- Test your feature-benefit with the, "So what?" test.
- Copywriting is the art and skill of writing in a manner that persuades and seduces your reader toward an action, viewpoint, opinion, or sale.
- When copywriting, use customer-centric words and phrases to describe your product or service, and avoid words like "we," "my," "us," and "our"; instead, use words like "you" and "your."
- Social proof: When people are unsure what to do, they mimic the actions of others.
- Multiple-source effect: When multiple different sources are cited, each individual source is perceived as having more influence.
- Frequently asked questions (FAQs) are your digital opportunity to handle objections.
- Putting the primary call-to-action in a button will add the visual queue that indicates "what to do next."
- The most important number to track when assessing the Engage & Educate component is conversion rate.

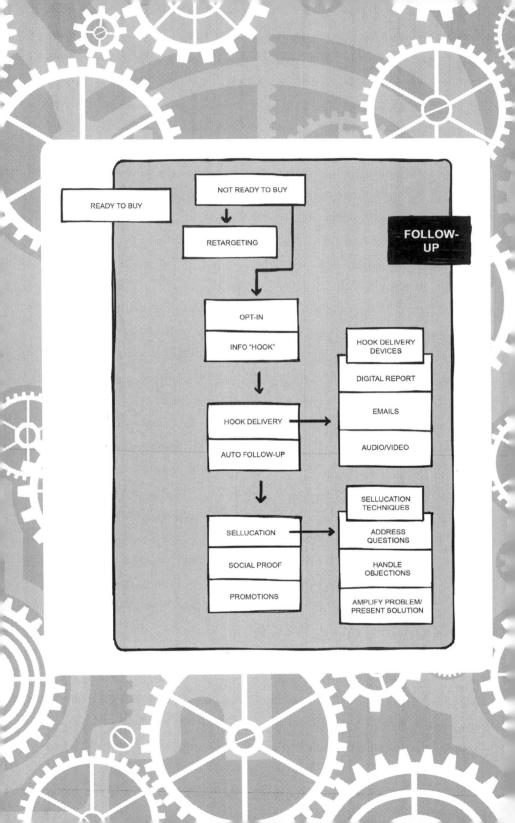

FOLLOW-UP

*Continue a dialogue with your prospects and politely
follow up so that no business slips through the cracks.*

"But won't I sacrifice our signature personalized sales experience?" one of our clients, a well-established yacht brokerage, skeptically inquired. This client had eschewed digital marketing for the last decade under the pretense that they didn't want to treat their fickle, high-net-worth clients "like a number."

Our client's marketing approach consisted of hosting posh yachting rendezvous and exclusive soirées. The attendees, wealthy retired men in their "golden years," appreciated a high-touch, low-pressure sales experience. The yachting courtship often lasted years before prospects felt comfortable writing a multimillion-dollar check.

When sales were stagnant for a few years, the client blamed it on the economy. But when the economy had recovered and sales started slumping, they got nervous and knew they had to do something to reverse the trend.

The yachting brokerage was racking up catering bills of caviar and Cristal but was inexplicably stuck in the longest sales dry spell in memory. In an attempt to turn things around, they planned the soirée of the century, bigger and more expensive than ever before. However, having not sold a megayacht for months, their coffers were just about drained, and they worried they might have to cancel the event.

Having heard a prospective yacht buyer brag about his son being on the *Shark Tank* and how growth hacking had revolutionized his business, the yacht-brokerage owner immediately reached out to us. The owner made two clear demands, "Whatever you do, it has to feel personalized... and it absolutely has to result in a yacht sale in the next eight weeks before the soirée."

This was no small task. How do you make thousands of persnickety prospects each feel as if his shopping experience is completely tailored to him, using nothing but digital marketing technology?

For this challenge, success hinged on our ability to design a digital Follow-Up process. The multimillion-dollar question was, would it produce a sale fast enough to save the soirée and, ultimately, the company?

HACKING THE FOLLOW-UP PROCESS

With even the most engaging and educating online sales experience, on average, ninety-seven out of one hundred prospects aren't going to take an immediate purchase action. However, those ninety-seven prospects came to you for a reason, and it's your duty and obligation to stay in front of them until they're prepared to make a purchase.

The challenge with offline follow-up is that things inevitably slip through the cracks. The moment you introduce a human being into a process, you create more opportunities for error. Whether it's poor organization or bad tracking, limitations of time and energy, a shift in prioritization, or a simple memory failure, there are many factors that can and do derail the analog world's follow-up process.

A digitized Follow-Up process can avoid the analog world's pitfalls and perils. There are ample tools at your disposal that help sequence, organize, and automate your Follow-Up process. For example, you can use an autoresponder to send a series of emails addressed with the prospect's first name that changes the message sequence and timing based on whether the prospect opened the prior email or clicked on a certain link. The same autoresponder principle is possible with every other communication medium you can think of, from text messages to phone calls to social media messages and more.

The benefit of digitizing your Follow-Up process is that it can happen automatically without you having to think about it; you can "set it and forget it." In fact, certain tactics allow you to follow up without the prospect giving you a single bit of contact information.

ADVERTISING RULE OF 7

The fundamental principle behind the value in instituting the Follow-Up component is repetition. The question we are often asked is, "How many times should I follow-up?" While the answer depends on your price point, sales cycle length, competitiveness of your industry, branding, and several other factors, the rule of thumb we cite is the Advertising Rule of 7. The Advertising Rule of 7 states that it takes approximately seven touch points for someone to be able to recall your brand.

The basis of the Advertising Rule of 7 is a 1956 Princeton University study done by cognitive psychologist George

> THE ADVERTISING RULE
> OF 7 STATES THAT IT TAKES
> APPROXIMATELY SEVEN TOUCH
> POINTS FOR SOMEONE TO BE
> ABLE TO RECALL YOUR BRAND.

Miller. Miller's Law states that the number of objects the average person can hold in working memory is 7 ± 2. Conveniently, the number of digits in a local US phone number is 7 (not until mobile phones were widely adopted were area codes commonly needed). Allegedly, movie studios targeted seven consumer touch points as early as the 1930s when wooing people to see their films.

Regardless of the origin, the primary takeaway from the Advertising Rule of 7 is that it takes repetition to be remembered. No one better internalized and executed this concept than the propagandists of the Second World War. By overtaking media outlets, they repeated their dogma until it permeated and intoxicated entire national belief systems. While the product of propaganda may have been undesirable, one cannot refute the influential power of repetition.

Fortunately, repetition in the digital world doesn't require commandeering a media outlet, and the results can be just as potent. In the following sections we will outline the basic structure for building an effective Follow-Up.

MAP IT TO YOUR SALES CYCLE

While the Advertising Rule of 7 provides a general sense of quantity, the next question we are often asked is about follow-up frequency. The framework we advise is to map your Follow-Up to your average sales cycle length. In general, the larger the dollar value of your product or service, the longer the sales cycle, particularly for business-to-consumer sales. If, for example, you've observed it takes an average of four weeks for someone to purchase your service, build your Follow-Up around a four-week period of time. We also advise front-loading your follow-up frequency to the beginning of the period to take advantage of the psychological principle knows as the primacy effect: the first touch points are more often remembered than the middle touch points and prospects are more open to communication. When you build out a follow-up sequence that extends the full length of your average sales cycle, you also benefit from the recency effect: the most recent correspondence will have more weight than all prior communication.

We are often asked questions like, "How much information should I ask for from a prospect? Should I ask for just a name and email? Should I get a phone number and what they're interested in? Should I ask for where they heard about us?" Some experts will advise asking for more information, while others will advise asking for less information. Neither advice is wrong; it just depends on your scenario and circumstance.

The differences in the amount of information you ask for from a prospect can be broadly categorized as high-barrier versus low-friction requests. A high-barrier request for information will ask for many pieces of information in an attempt to produce more qualified leads; the more you know about a lead, the more qualified that lead is. The understanding here is that the more serious a prospect is about purchasing your good or service, the more inclined he will be to give you information. For companies that are plagued with low-quality lead flow and are concerned about conserving sales resources, asking for more information is a good approach.

For companies that are interested in maximizing lead flow and are comfortable handling a certain degree of low-quality leads, a low-friction request for information is an appropriate approach. In general, the more contact information you ask from the prospect, the more "friction" there is and the less likely the prospect will be to comply with your request.

A hybrid information-capture approach is to collect information during the follow-up process. For example, you can start with a low-friction name and email request and collect more lead intelligence as a prospect engages with your material through subsequent questionnaires. However, collecting information as time goes on requires a

"

...MAP YOUR
FOLLOW-UP TO YOUR
AVERAGE SALES
CYCLE LENGTH.

more robust system capable of patching together lead information over time. As such, the hybrid approach is generally something companies evolve into after first implementing a simpler solution.

Many companies are quick to dismiss the value of acquiring an email address. "Who would want another digital newsletter?" they ask. "People don't read their emails anymore!" they exclaim. Given that email is used for critical communication such as online banking, flight information, and online shopping updates, it's unlikely to be replaced any time soon. As it relates to whether people want a newsletter, the answer is that most people do not. However, for many purchases there is a research phase that consumers undergo, and it's a value-added service to be the company that provides education. Among the many ways to deliver consumer education, email is the most cost-effective. If you sell something that does not have a research phase, you can incentivize individuals with a discount. Regardless of the incentive or information you provide, a database of qualified prospects has significant tangible value.

The primary value in building a database of prospects is two-fold. For companies that experience seasonality or cyclicality, a single message broadcasted to your list of leads can help you control the ups and downs of your business. Additionally, as you release new products and services, you will have an immediate audience to tap into. In fact, we've worked with companies that recruit passionate customers from their database to help provide feedback in the product-development process. The ability to control seasonality and have an audience to launch to has palpable value if you were to sell your business in the future. We've seen entire companies purchased for millions of dollars solely for their database of leads and customers.

THE PROCESS

Prior to designing the follow-up sequence, it's important to have a clear articulation of the brand voice. The voice is a set of rules for the writing produced by your brand and is a function of having an intimate understanding of your target audience. One can further assume that the individuals inclined to sign up to receive more follow-up information are going to be more responsive to logos-based (logic) rhetoric than the cohort of clients that make more pathos-based (emotion) decisions and purchase without needing to do deeper diligence.

Once the brand voice is clearly articulated, one can apply the 4 E's of Copywriting framework to craft messages that captivate and motivate. Broadly defined, the more "E's" you convey, the better:

THE 4 E'S OF COPYWRITING

- **Engaging**: *Is the content compelling and of interest to the reader?*
- **Educational**: *Is the content teaching the reader something relevant to your product or service?*
- **Entertaining**: *Would the reader enjoy reading your content?*
- **Emotional**: *Would your content stir up emotions inside your reader?*

The 4 E's framework serves as a solid mental checklist as you assess the potential impact and influence of your follow-up messaging. While it may not be necessary to touch on all four points all the time, the 4 E's framework gives you a self-assessment standard for building trust, authority, and rapport.

One common stumbling block during the construction of the follow-up process is coming up with topics to write about. As with the other components, ASP™ Follow-Up is a digital manifestation of an analog process that you already employ. Follow-up phone calls and direct mail to prospective buyers are the analog parallel to what can be replicated digitally. The framework we use as a starting point when building out a follow-up process is as follows:

FOLLOW-UP FRAMEWORK

- **Opt-In:** Offer a desirable bribe (also called a "hook" or "lead magnet") in exchange for an email address (at a minimum).

- **Hook Delivery:** Deliver what was promised for the prospect opting in. Digital delivery can range from digital reports to emails to audio or video content. The benefit of digital delivery is that you can provide immediate gratification to your prospect and it's free to send.

- **Sellucation:** Sellucation is selling through education. Each Follow-Up installment is an opportunity to address common questions, handle objections, and amplify the problem while presenting your solution. It's education with the implicit intent of driving sales.

- **Social Proof:** Reiterating the social proof you presented in the Engage & Educate phase with testimonials, reviews, awards, partner logos, and case studies will enhance your credibility and build trust.

- **Promotions:** Offering free consultations, discounts, and other incentives can motivate your prospect to take action. Communicating an expiration associated with the promotion can create a sense of urgency that further persuades prospects to move forward.

In summary, you are replicating a conversation that could conceivably take place face-to-face. You are educating your customer, handling objections, answering questions, and providing incentives for the prospect to take action.

EVEN WHEN YOU DON'T GET THEIR CONTACT INFO

Going back to our illustrative sample of one hundred website visitors, you may get three individuals to make a direct purchase and another three to opt in for your lead magnet and potentially purchase from you at a later date. Although that number may appear immaterial, assuming one out of those three leads who opted in purchases from you, you have increased your sales by 33 percent, which is not bad. The beautiful thing is, there is a way for you to stay in front of all your website visitors, even if they didn't give you their contact information. The way you stay in front of all your website visitors is with an advertising method called "retargeting" (also called "remarketing"). Retargeting enables you to get the frequency of impressions of a multibillion-dollar brand such as Coca-Cola without needing a multibillion-dollar advertising budget.

The way retargeting works is by identifying and remembering users, through their web browsers, who have visited your website and serving ads to those users as they browse other places on the web. Whether they're

WHETHER
THEY'RE PERUSING
A SOCIAL MEDIA SITE OR
READING THEIR FAVORITE
BLOG, RETARGETING ALLOWS
YOU TO TARGET YOUR ADS
SPECIFICALLY TO PEOPLE THAT
HAVE PREVIOUSLY VISITED
YOUR WEBSITE.

perusing a social media site or reading their favorite blog, retargeting allows you to target your ads specifically to people that have previously visited your website. This is powerful because it allows you to market specifically to individuals who have shown interest in your specific product or service and your brand.

Going back to the Advertising Rule of 7, retargeting ads are the key difference makers between someone remembering your brand and forgetting. The first brand impression may be a pay-per-click ad, the second brand impression would then be your website, and impressions three through seven would be from retargeting ads. You may assume that this powerful form of advertising would be extraordinarily expensive but unless you are getting more than ten thousand monthly visitors, your ad spend will probably be less than one hundred dollars a month. For most businesses with a local presence, monthly visitors range in the single-digit thousands, so this is a delightfully low-cost growth hack to implement.

Categorically, we make two main differentiations in retargeting ad units: brand-based and direct-response ad units. Intuitively, brand-based ad units convey your overall brand or company, and direct-response ad units focus on a specific product or service. Starting out, we advise launching brand-based ad units and retargeting

"

INTUITIVELY, BRAND-BASED
AD UNITS CONVEY YOUR
OVERALL BRAND OR COMPANY,
AND DIRECT-RESPONSE AD
UNITS FOCUS ON A SPECIFIC
PRODUCT OR SERVICE.

visitors that visit any page of your website. If you only offer a singular product or service, then you may be able to experiment with direct-response style ads targeted to all visitors. Otherwise, for those companies that have more than ten thousand monthly visitors and offer multiple products or services, you can get more granular and retarget to people that visited specific pages. For example, if you were a roofer that also provides solar installation, you could serve solar ads to a prospect that visited the solar page of your website.

GROWTH HACKTIC

One way of cutting down your retargeting ad bill is through "pixel burning." For websites that have a payment portal online, such as e-commerce sites, you can isolate those who have completed payments and remove those individuals from the retargeting population since they have already completed the desired action.

GROWTH HACKING APPLIED

As we investigated the situation, the yacht brokerage's slumping sales seemed to correlate directly to the reduction in the broker head count. The brokers make their money on commission, and the static sales caused a couple brokers to seek employment elsewhere.

When we spoke with the remaining brokers, they talked about how busy they were following up with thousands of prospects in their Rolodex, especially as they assumed responsibility for the prospects previously handled by the departed brokers.

When we asked the brokers, "Which prospects are the most important ones?" they curtly replied, "They're all important." When we modified the question by inquiring, "Which prospects are most likely to buy in the next eight weeks before the soirée?" Again they replied, "They're all equally likely to buy; they buy when they're ready."

If all the prospects were equally important and equally likely to buy, we needed to build a way for the brokers to politely and unobtrusively follow up multiple times in advance of the soirée in order to maximize the likelihood of a sale taking place. Simply put, the brokers needed leverage.

The first thing we implemented was an autoresponder email campaign. In our conversations with the yacht brokers, we compiled perfect answers to all the frequently asked questions and common objections. We also crafted customer stories that conveyed the yachting dream life. To complement the autoresponder technology, we implemented a robust retargeting display ad campaign that kept the brokerage's brand name in front of the potential customers practically every time they browsed online.

As a result, the yacht brokerage didn't just sell one yacht before the soirée; they sold multiple. At the event, a recent yacht buyer went up to our client and told him, "I kept seeing your yacht ads everywhere, and I took that as a sign that some higher power was telling me it was time to finally pull the trigger and purchase a yacht." With that one comment, the yacht brokerage owner instantly converted from a growth-hacking skeptic to a growth-hacking disciple. The implementation of the Follow-Up resulted in a record-setting sales year for the brokerage and helped put them on a sales trajectory that shows no signs of slowing. Even more impressive, the record-setting sales year was accomplished without hiring a single additional employee.

FOLLOW-UP TAKEAWAYS

- The Advertising Rule of 7 states that it takes approximately seven touch points for someone to be able to recall your brand.
- Map your Follow-Up to your average sales cycle length.
- The more information you request from your lead, the more "friction" there is, which leads to the prospect being less likely to provide the requested information.
- Apply the 4 E's of Copywriting framework to craft messages that captivate and motivate: Engaging, Educational, Entertaining, and Emotional.
- Retargeting allows you to target your ads specifically to people that have previously visited your website.
- Brand-based ad units convey your overall brand or company, and direct-response ad units focus on a specific product or service.

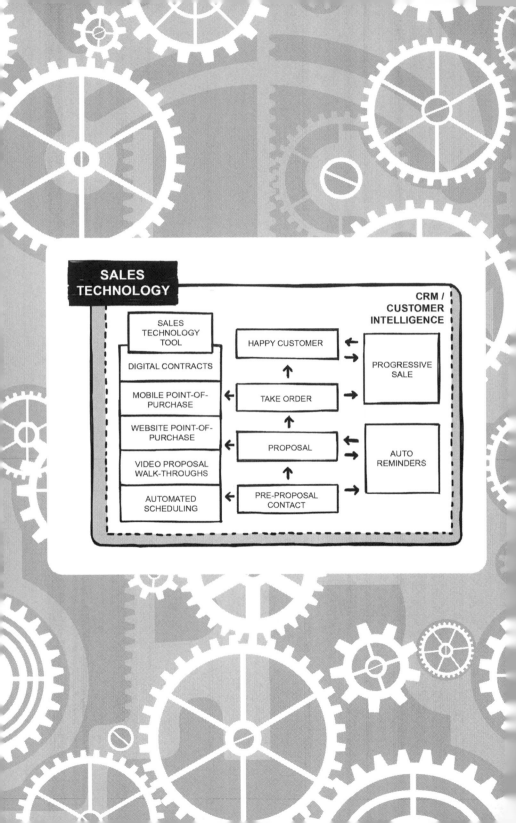

SALES TECHNOLOGY

Use an arsenal of tools that makes it easy for you to close sales while identifying opportunities to upsell your clients when they are in the mood to buy.

For six months we had overhauled and scaled out their Attraction, First Impression, Engage & Educate, and Follow-Up. The result for our client, a chain of a half-dozen brick-and-mortar medical clinics, was an impressive 50 percent increase in revenue.

The client was over-the-moon excited about the unprecedented growth and had inked plans to open up two more clinics by the end of the year. The new facilities required a significant upfront investment, but they signed the lease contracts, purchased the equipment, and hired the new staff without blinking an eye because growth hacking had revolutionized their business and put them on a rocket-ship trajectory.

Just as the ink was drying on the two six-figure lease agreements, the growth rate came to a screeching stop. It was as if someone had flipped the growth switch off, and the business hit a plateau. The client was panicked; they had lease payments, equipment installments, and payroll to make. If they didn't continue growing, they would be stuck with payments they simply couldn't afford. We immediately jumped in and began methodically troubleshooting the situation.

Was there no more room for patients at the clinics? We examined the utilization rates, and they were operating at a healthy 75 to 80 percent utilization, which meant there was still room for growth.

Was there no more ad inventory available? We examined Attraction, and there was still plenty of search traffic, and a recent test with online radio indicated that there was a ton of opportunity with radio advertising as well.

The Patient Relations Director was anxious for us to reignite growth as he was about to hire an Associate Director to help him handle the influx of prospective patients but had paused his efforts until the growth rate returned. This seemingly small comment was actually a key clue for solving the growth problem.

We spent time learning about the role and responsibilities the Associate Director would fill. Essentially, the Patient Relations Director was overburdened with prospective patients, and there weren't enough hours in the day to keep up with the prospects. He spent most of his day making calls, but only one in twenty-five prospective patient calls picked up. To make matters worse, he was working overtime tracking all his correspondence manually in an Excel sheet that was ballooning out of control.

We were confident that Sales Technology could replace the need to hire an Associate Director, whose job was to prequalify patient leads for the Director and manually enter patient information into the spreadsheet, and do so at a fraction of the cost. The client was skeptical that implementing Sales Technology would bring back their former growth rate, but we had built up enough trust over the last six months that they gave us the green light to proceed.

If Sales Technology didn't fix the client's growth problems, our client would have wasted the last of their cash reserves and would potentially need to shut down the new locations as quickly as they opened. Our growth-hacking reputation and the client's continued success rested completely on Sales Technology.

THE PRINCIPLES OF SALES TECHNOLOGY

The starting point for what to do online begins with an inspection of what is already happening offline. The analog to digital parallels vary industry to industry and company to company, but it's safe to assume that your offline sales process provides a better client experience than your online sales process. As such, there are ample opportunities to take what is working offline and apply that online.

An example of a process that generally occurs offline but is often overlooked online is the process of upsells and cross-sells. Both upsells and cross-sells help you increase the average order value per client, which increases revenue without increasing ad expense. Fortunately, both upsells and cross-sells can be easily accomplished online, thanks to various Sales Technology tools. To understand the difference between the two, upsells "up" the price by suggesting a more premium product or service, and cross-sells encourage you to reach across the aisle and add a complementary product to your order. For many businesses we work with, simply adding cross-sell pur-

> ...UPSELLS "UP" THE PRICE BY SUGGESTING A MORE PREMIUM PRODUCT OR SERVICE, AND CROSS-SELLS ENCOURAGE YOU TO REACH ACROSS THE AISLE AND ADD A COMPLEMENTARY PRODUCT TO YOUR ORDER.

chase recommendations or a one-click upsell into the online checkout process dramatically increases revenue.

We recognize that not all goods or services can be purchased online with a click of a button. In those instances, there are still several opportunities to inject conveniences into the sales process. For example, if a purchase requires an in-person consultation, there are online tools that sync to your calendar in real-time to enable prospects to book a consultation even if they're perusing your site at 2:00 a.m. on a Saturday. If your consultation occurs at a client's location, there are ways for you to bring the point-of-purchase with you on a mobile device. If you are unable to provide an immediate estimate, there are tools for providing video-proposal walk-throughs that alert you when your prospect is engaging as well as tools for facilitating immediate digital-contract execution. The suite of sales tools you select will depend on your industry and business model, but the process starts with inspecting your current real-world process and asking yourself, "How can I digitize this?"

The burden of investigating what you should digitize and how you should digitize isn't fully dependent on an introspective analysis. Assessing your competitors can quickly reveal tools that you can directly apply to your digital business processes. It may be as simple as making a test purchase and observing the tools your competition uses in

"

THE SUITE OF SALES
TOOLS YOU SELECT
WILL DEPEND ON YOUR
INDUSTRY AND BUSINESS MODEL,
BUT THE PROCESS STARTS WITH
INSPECTING YOUR CURRENT REAL-
WORLD PROCESS AND ASKING
YOURSELF, "HOW CAN I
DIGITIZE THIS?"

the sales process. Alternatively, attending industry events provides a forum for idea exchange and best-practice sharing. Additionally, you may want to consider observing and talking with companies in adjacent industries, as sales processes often vary only marginally from industry to industry and certain industries are quicker to adopt new technology than others. In general, the more competitive the industry, the more likely industry participants are to quickly adopt new technology.

If you operate in a highly complex industry or there are few easily observable competitors, it can be valuable to engage an outside consultant to help guide your company through the technology identification and adoption process. Make sure to have the consultant provide an estimate around expected sales efficiency improvements and justify their fees in terms of directly attributable return on investment. A good consultant will candidly provide insight as to whether you are a good fit and provide solid advice, regardless of whether you engage or not.

In certain cases, you may need to string together several technologies in a unique way in order to accomplish the desired task. The stringing together of technologies is often less burdensome than one would anticipate. The vast majority of off-the-shelf technologies are designed with Application Programming Interfaces (APIs) that make it easy for one technology to "talk" with another. In fact, there are tools such as Zapier that are exclusively designed to plug one application's APIs into another. For example, an inbound email from a new prospect can trigger an automatic entry into a spreadsheet that logs all your leads. Or a sales-order form entry can automatically trigger a thank-you text message to be sent out. While the combinations and permutations of stringing together various technologies are vast, you may still encounter a situation where there is nothing that fulfills your specific needs. A regular marketer will hit the wall and wait for sales technology to catch up at some point in the future. A growth hacker will embrace the opportunity to create a technological competitive sales advantage and roll up her sleeves and build the tool herself.

We have built several proprietary tools at Deviate Labs, and the process is not nearly as complicated or painful as one may expect. The reality is, even when you are building a tool "from scratch," there are large repositories of code that developers will be able to swipe and leverage when creating the tool. Furthermore, there are plenty of freelance hiring platforms that help you identify and contract a developer with the required expertise. Building a Sales Technology tool from scratch doesn't require starting from ground zero or even knowing how to code. It requires identifying the right repositories, frameworks, and developers.

CUSTOMER RELATIONSHIP MANAGEMENT

One of the most foundational sales technologies is a customer-relationship management tool (CRM). A CRM is a technology platform that manages the information associated with your clients. The analog offline parallel is the Rolodex. The digitization of the Rolodex enabled business owners to keep track of their contacts (e.g., prospects and customers) and also jot down whatever helpful notes they deem appropriate. But the Rolodex analogy hardly does the modern CRM justice, as CRMs do far more than just house client information. The modern CRM aggregates data across the multitude of client-acquisition tools and Sales Technology tools and brings the right information to light at the right time in ways that are often fully automated.

The many varieties and configurations of client-acquisition tools and Sales Technology tools have led to a number of different "species" of CRMs that have evolved to fit various industries. Attempts at building a one-size-fits-all CRM, such as Salesforce, inevitably reach a point of feature bloat and lead to user confusion when they try to be too many things to too many people. The CRM that will work best for you is a highly personal decision that is dependent on what you use it for. Compatibility and usability will be your two core considerations when selecting a CRM. It needs to connect all your current tools in a

"

A REGULAR MARKETER WILL
HIT THE WALL AND WAIT FOR
SALES TECHNOLOGY TO CATCH
UP AT SOME POINT IN THE FUTURE.
A GROWTH HACKER WILL EMBRACE
THE OPPORTUNITY TO CREATE A
TECHNOLOGICAL COMPETITIVE SALES
ADVANTAGE AND ROLL UP HER SLEEVES
AND BUILD THE TOOL HERSELF.

way that is user-friendly enough for you and your team to understand. CRM switching costs are high as accumulated data may not port over to competing solutions, so choose wisely.

As important as it is to choose wisely, balance that with the fact that there is no "perfect" solution. Each CRM is going to have some wrinkles and blemishes that you may have to iron, polish, or just live with. While a certain degree of your assessment will be the calculus of how the CRM fits with your current systems and processes, another part of your assessment is what new things your CRM enables. A great CRM will enable you to do new things to drive revenue and improve your ability to provide an excellent customer experience.

GROWTH HACKING APPLIED

After implementing the first four components of the ASP™, the chain of medical clinics grew at an unprecedented rate, 50 percent in six months, which proved to be more than their old sales systems and processes could handle. Specifically, the Patient Relations Director was having difficulty keeping track of all the prospective patients, and the customer care the company was known for was starting to falter. Although it's a high-class problem, they had fallen victim to their own success.

> THE CRM THAT WILL WORK
> BEST FOR YOU IS A HIGHLY
> PERSONAL DECISION THAT IS
> DEPENDENT ON WHAT YOU USE IT FOR.
> COMPATIBILITY AND USABILITY WILL
> BE YOUR TWO CORE CONSIDERATIONS
> WHEN SELECTING A CRM. IT NEEDS TO
> CONNECT ALL YOUR CURRENT TOOLS
> IN A WAY THAT IS USER-FRIENDLY
> ENOUGH FOR YOU AND YOUR
> TEAM TO UNDERSTAND.

We immediately identified a customer-relationship management system that would address all the pain points the Patient Relations Director was experiencing and, if implemented correctly, eliminate the need to hire an Associate Director. An additional pain point we hoped to address was advertising attribution. When the old system was in place, the client only had one paid marketing initiative, so attribution was not a concern. However, when we launched three new Attraction initiatives, things were much harder to track.

Among many benefits of the new sales technology, one that was not possible with the old system was the ability to automate patient appointments and send reminders in the form of emails, calls, and text messages. With the old system, the Patient Relations Director was also responsible for reminding patients about their appointments and following up whenever someone missed. The added administrative burden associated with each patient was taking away from the activities that generated revenue. With the new sales technology in place, the Director was able to focus his time on the highest value tasks, and the patients received an even better client experience than before.

The results from the Sales Technology implementation were better than expected. The client was able to keep the new locations open, the growth rate returned, and their bottom-line profit expanded as they were able to grow without the typical growing pain of having to hire and train a new employee.

SALES TECHNOLOGY TAKEAWAYS

- Upsells vs. cross-sells: Upsells "up" the price by suggesting a more premium product or service, and cross-sells encourage you to reach across the aisle and add a complementary product to your order.
- The suite of sales tools you select will depend on your industry and business model, but the process starts with inspecting your current real-world process and asking yourself, "How can I digitize this?"
- A regular marketer will hit the wall and wait for sales technology to catch up at some point in the future. A growth hacker will embrace the opportunity to create a technological competitive sales advantage and roll up her sleeves and build the tool herself.
- The CRM that will work best for you is a highly personal decision that is dependent on what you use it for. Compatibility and usability will be your two core considerations when selecting a CRM. It needs to connect all your current tools in a way that is user-friendly enough for you and your team to understand.

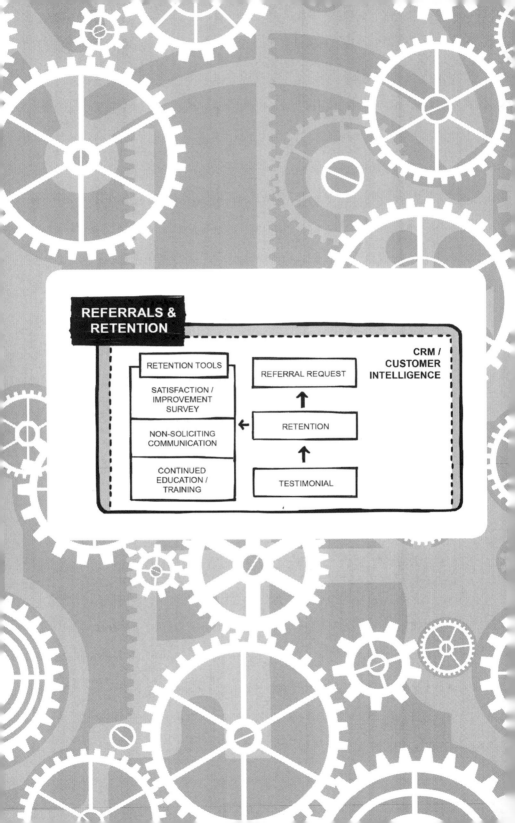

REFERRALS & RETENTION

CRM / CUSTOMER INTELLIGENCE

RETENTION TOOLS

SATISFACTION / IMPROVEMENT SURVEY

NON-SOLICITING COMMUNICATION

CONTINUED EDUCATION / TRAINING

REFERRAL REQUEST

RETENTION

TESTIMONIAL

REFERRALS & RETENTION

Generate high-value referrals and spread the positive words from your happy clients like wildfire to heat up your cold prospects and send eye-catching signals to your new ones.

Our prospective client, a start-up boutique child-development center in Boston, had done everything they could think of to increase enrollment. In Boston, it's not uncommon for affluent parents to register their unborn children for preschools that often cost as much as college tuition. Therefore, it's no small task to get a parent to leave the queue of one school and take a risk on a new and unproven institution.

As experienced operators of some of the most prestigious child-education institutions on the East Coast, the founders spared no expense when advertising the grand opening of their new facility. The founders were well aware that if they didn't launch at or near full capacity, they would risk having to shut the center down at the end of the first semester, as parents would quickly lose faith and pull their children.

The development center burned through a massive prelaunch marketing budget that included mommy blogger write-ups, open-house events, tons of social media ads, and even prescreen commercials at all the local theaters. Despite the big marketing splash, the development center opened its doors with 50 percent enrollment and was operating at a loss in order to keep the school open. If they didn't increase enrollment in the next semester, they would be forced to close their doors as quickly as they opened.

The client was in dire straits when they called us. They had no money left for advertising, and they needed to double enrollment in the next three and half months.

With no money to spend on advertising, how were we going to growth hack our way out of this situation?

They appeared to have done everything right. They spent tons of money on Attraction, First Impression was solid, their website had 80 percent of what we needed for Engage & Educate, Follow-Up was in place, and they had implemented all the latest Sales Technology in the education industry.

The only component missing was Referrals & Retention, but as a start-up child-development facility that was only a month old, would this really make a difference?

We believed so. Our client, out of options, gave us full authority to do whatever we could to save the center.

GETTING OTHERS TO MARKET FOR YOU

Referrals & Retention has been fertile ground for many of the most effective growth hacks in history. In the A Brief History section of the Introduction, we highlighted the incentivized referral programs implemented by both PayPal and Dropbox that brought in hundreds of millions of dollars in sales. The word-of-mouth referral analog is a significant sales contributor for the vast majority of businesses. The irony is that word-of-mouth referrals work so well that business owners overlook referrals as an opportunity for driving growth. Instead of spending ad dollars on a one-off TV ad campaign, you could apply those same dollars to the digitization and incentivization of your referral process, which can result in an immediate and permanent lift in sales.

The difference between an active referral system and a passive referral system is often the singular difference between a static company and a high-growth company. The businesses that provide an exceptional product or service generally enjoy a meaningful amount of organically occurring word-of-mouth referrals. In fact, many businesses we work with are entirely sustained by referrals, and when they approach us looking for growth opportunities, they're surprised when our first recommendation is to "get more referrals." Despite having the confidence that they provide the best product in town, they're comatosely timid when it comes to actively asking for referrals. However, with a little reprogramming of their psychology, we are able to unlock a treasure trove of cost-effective growth hacks.

Given that you are the best at what you do in your area, you deserve the most amount of business. In fact, not only do you deserve the business, but your clients deserve the opportunity to help their friends and family get the same excellent service they received from you. In a passive system, you are forced to rely on your clients to remember and convey the right information at the right time. In an active system, you give your clients the tools so they don't have to remember all the right information, and you provide them with an incentive so that they can create the right timing. In The Process section below, we will elaborate on the specific tools and incentives that will transform your referral process from passive to active.

In the Attraction chapter, we discussed the barter tactic we used to land our *Shark Tank* companies as clients without spending any money on marketing. At the core of the barter arrangement was our active referral system. We were so confident in our ability to provide excellent service that we made referrals a condition of doing business with us: the "payment" for our service. If we would have passively relied on the reciprocal good nature of our first *Shark Tank* client to refer us if we did a good job, we may have landed another client or two, but because we formally asked, our client formally sought referrals, and we ended up receiving a half dozen clients as a result.

CUSTOMER LIFETIME VALUE

Lifetime value (LTV) is a term we first introduced in the Becoming Resource Rich section in chapter 0 of this book, recounting the circumstances in which Box raised a war chest of investment capital to double down on growth. When LTV is greater than the customer acquisition cost (CAC), you can justify spending a lot of money on sales and marketing. The Attraction chapter was dedicated to hacking growth by reducing the cost of acquiring a customer. This chapter is dedicated to hacking growth by increasing the lifetime value of your customer through retention.

For many of the businesses we work with, it's a better use of resources to sell more goods and services to an existing customer than to go out and acquire a new customer. The objection we are often faced with by our clients is, "I have nothing else to sell my former clients." To use that same roofing company as an example, adding a simple maintenance program or adding a solar installation service can dramatically increase the lifetime customer value, which in turn allows the roofing business to justify spending more money on customer acquisition. This opens up new channels that their roofing-only competitors simply can't afford since their LTV would be less than their CAC.

THE PROCESS

TESTIMONIALS

Testimonials are a key piece of social proof that feeds the Engage & Educate and Follow-Up components of the ASP™. Given that testimonials can provide valuable insight into what is going well with your product or service, it is best practice to make testimonial requests a permanent part of your sales process. In certain industries where price is negotiable, you can make a practice of providing a "success story" discount in exchange for giving the testimonial. This implies that they will be a noteworthy success and primes them for providing a positive review.

In industries where the "success story" tactic is not a good fit, it is best practice to time your testimonial request with the moment of peak happiness. The formula we employ to engineer engaging testimonials is as follows:

TESTIMONIAL FORMULA

[Specific End Result or Benefit the Customer Received] + [Specific Period of Time] + [Accompanied Customer Emotion] + [Customer Name with Relevant Stats]

Example: I was craving a Hawaiian style pizza at one in the morning and was stoked when it arrived just twenty minutes after I called! ~Chad R., Pasadena, CA

While the formula provides a good structure for presenting your testimonials, it's naïve to assume your customers will be waxing poetic testimonials that fit that construct perfectly. It can be good to aggregate some free-form testimonials, but in most cases the quality of your testimonials will be improved by asking the right questions. Here are some directed questions that should help you tease out solid testimonials from your clients:

TESTIMONIAL QUESTIONS

1. *What were you looking for when you found [COMPANY]?*
2. *What compelled you to choose [COMPANY] over others?*
3. *What results did you get from working with [COMPANY]?*
4. *When [COMPANY] [COMPLETED SOLUTION], what did you like most about the experience?*
5. *Who else would you recommend [COMPANY] to?*

Inevitably you will have some customers that are difficult to please and will have negative experiences with your product. Those individuals are not going to be the ones to voluntarily provide a glowing testimonial. They're the ones that are likely to resort to a review site to blow off some steam. To some extent you can attempt to preempt negative commentary through satisfaction surveys and other internal feedback forms, but it's impossible to ward off all negativity.

We have countless clients who attempt to ignore the bad behavior of the vocal minority that resort to take-down commentary on review sites and social media. The problem with that approach is that prospective clients that seek counsel from review sites and social media will get an overindexed negative perception of your business because of the vocal minority. Therefore, your approach to review sites and social media ought to be to control the conversation about your company... or someone else will.

One of the key benefits of making testimonial requests a permanent part of your sales process is that you can funnel individuals to one of the many review sites or social media platforms that your prospects could potentially come across. When negative comments do exist, you are able to dilute down the negativity with the positive commentary. Nevertheless, you still cannot ignore the negative comments. The framework we recommend for addressing negative comments is as follows:

HOW TO HANDLE NEGATIVE COMMENTARY	
NEGATIVE TRUTH	**NEGATIVE LIE**
1. Admit 2. Apologize 3. Promote the opposite	1. State the comment is inaccurate or invalid 2. Substantiate your comment

"Promoting the opposite" of a negative true comment often means explaining how you are remedying it or addressing the problem in a way that it's believably unlikely for a future client to experience a similar issue. For example, if a client had a bad experience with a sales member, you can talk about how that individual is no longer with the team or how you have taken measures to ensure that the team member will no longer make a similar mistake.

As it relates to a negative lie, it isn't uncommon to have competitors slinging mud or miserly clients seeking financial retribution for a wrong that never occurred. In either case, it is worth seeking a judgment from the review platform or social media site to see if you can get a ruling so that the negative false comment can be removed. In cases where people are seeking money, a small settlement where the comment is removed in exchange for a modest monetary value may be a worthwhile investment, as frustrating as the extortion situation may feel.

Once a negative comment has been addressed, it's always worth your time to politely ask the individual to remove, change, or append to their negative remarks if he feels the issue has been sufficiently resolved. In many cases, a pragmatic and proactive approach will set you apart from the vast majority of faceless and negligent enterprises out there and be appreciated by the author of the negative review.

Companies are no longer faceless, soulless entities that

> **...CONTROL THE CONVERSATION ABOUT YOUR COMPANY... OR SOMEONE ELSE WILL.**

are hiding in some gigantic office building, unreachable to the masses. Social media and modern review sites have brought the character, integrity, and reputation of every business to the public eye. Controlling the conversation around your business will enable you to control your destiny.

RETENTION

As mentioned in the Customer Lifetime Value section above, often the best use of your growth-hacking resources is to increase the LTV of your customer by improving retention. In the Sales Technology section, we discussed ways to increase your average order value through upsells and cross-sells at a single point in time. In this section we will discuss how to expand the duration of the relationship with your customer and increase the opportunities for repeat purchases.

For industries that sell higher dollar-value discretionary purchases that have an element of luxury or leisure, you will often see special interest clubs and events used to foster a community and lifestyle around the brand. If you fall into that luxury or leisure category, then you are most likely already doing something of that nature. The opportunities often lie in taking the offline community you have cultivated and bringing components of that online. Self-contained forums have evolved into social media groups, and we are often asked what format we recommend. The first recommendation is that we advise selecting only one format because having multiple formats multiplies your work at the expense of the community quality. The second recommendation is to select a social platform where your audience is already spending time. If or when your selected social platform falls out of favor, we advise porting that community to a forum you control on your website, assuming you have developed a critical mass of followers, so you don't have to keep porting your audience every time social-platform preferences change.

We mentioned satisfaction surveys as a preemptive tactic for reducing negative commentary on review and social sites, but satisfaction surveys can also play a role in improving retention. Certain questions can be sales opportunities in disguise. For example, a question after a residential roofing project could be, "Were you aware of our discounted roofing maintenance programs that automatically extend the satisfaction guarantee on your new roof?" The survey can serve as a participative checklist that ensures your client's needs were fully addressed. The responses to your questions can reveal new revenue opportunities, enable you to fix oversights in your process, and serve as the basis for client "win-back" campaigns where you woo recently churned clients back with various incentives.

Although we are conditioned to "always be closing," there is something refreshingly effective about agenda-free, nonsoliciting client communication. A simple holiday hello or birthday well-wish can often convert better than the world's best copywritten direct-mail piece.

GROWTH HACKTIC

If you plan on sending holiday greetings or something similar, send them on an "off" holiday. For example, a "Happy Saint Patrick's Day" card will be more distinctive and more likely to be read than a New Year "Happy Holidays" card. We worked with one of our clients to send a box of See's chocolates for Valentine's Day to their top general contractor clients, and they ended up generating more than fifty thousand dollars of contracts from a two-hundred-dollar investment. They also helped several "forgetful" gentlemen look like wonderfully thoughtful husbands when they brought chocolate to their wives on Valentine's Day.

For many products and services, there is an element of education or training that accompanies the sale. For clients that have retention problems, the solution most often resides in the postsale education-and-training component.

For example, there is a technology company that makes a thermometer for server rooms that alerts you if things get too hot. They sold the device at a low cost as the profit was in the alert subscription service; however, despite the tech-savvy users, a ton of people purchased the product and never set it up, which meant they never subscribed. So, the company made a simple video clip of a regular UPS guy setting up the product in less than one minute. Retention skyrocketed, and revenue grew more than 60 percent. What may seem like an obvious or simple process to you may be more intimidating to your users than you ever imagined.

While top-of-funnel Attraction tactics typically capture the lion's share of a marketer's attention, some of the best growth-hacking opportunities are after the point of initial purchase at the very bottom of the proverbial funnel. Retention improvements are particularly potent for early-stage companies and mature companies that have not recently spent time optimizing the retention process. Improving customer lifetime value by increasing retention improvements has a large but still finite opportunity for growth. The next section will discuss referrals, which have, by comparison, an infinite opportunity for growth.

We've established the conceptual difference between a passive and an active referral system. Once you have ideologically adopted an active referral system, you are tasked with determining which system will best suit your business. The two primary categories of active referral systems are financial and in-kind. To illustrate the difference between the two systems, a financial incentive would be to give a referral source twenty dollars cash, whereas an in-kind incentive would be to give a referral source a product or service of yours that is valued at twenty dollars.

In general, an in-kind referral system is a superior choice, as your cost of providing the good or service is presumably less than the perceived value. This was the core takeaway from the Dropbox case study in the Introduction. One additional characteristic that Dropbox had that made it more effective was dualistic incentives, meaning that both the giver and the recipient derived a benefit. Both in-kind and financial incentive systems can employ this same dualistic tactic.

In certain industries, in-kind referrals are not feasible, and financial incentives are the next best alternative. The common financial incentive systems are cash, or some of form of currency such as loyalty points, and discounts. In transactions with large organizations that have committee-based decisions or industries where financial incentives are restricted, a charitable donation provides an incentive at arm's reach that can be a sufficient motivator to make a referral.

One system that doesn't fit in either the in-kind or financial incentive categories that can have a dramatic effect is referrals as a condition of doing business. In other words, there is no incentive besides the client getting the privilege of working with you. Referrals as a condition of doing business work well when you truly have a well-differentiated offering and are requested with absolute conviction. You may run across this with high-end consultants, but it's a fairly rare system. When referrals as a condition of doing business works, it's a crazy cost-effective growth hack, as you will likely not need to spend a dollar more on marketing ever again.

GROWTH HACKING APPLIED

After the child-development center made a huge marketing splash but was only at 50 percent enrollment, they were faced with the prospect of having to shut the facility down. Such a situation would have been a professional embarrassment for the founders who left senior positions at competing facilities and a letdown to the families that had trusted them to take care of their children.

Coming into a situation where virtually all Attraction

channels had been exhausted and there was no money to spend on advertising felt like we were destined to fail. However, we had worked with a company in a completely different industry that encountered a similar situation, and we were able to turn things around. The missing piece of the puzzle lay in referrals, getting the parents who enrolled their children to help motivate the missing 50 percent.

Our referral growth-hacking hypothesis was based on parallels we drew from working with, of all things, an LA nightclub. Club promoters coupled with arbitrary line queues get the first 50 percent of the club filled, but the second 50 percent comes from individuals posting to social media and texting their friends to join them—in other words, referrals.

In a club, one of the moments of peak happiness is right when the velvet rope opens up and lets you in. The immediate prompt is a photo opportunity against a backdrop branded with the club's logo, so all your friends and followers know exactly where you are at. The next moment of peak happiness is when you are a couple drinks in and taking a break to catch up on social media while in line at the restroom. Again, this is a perfect opportunity to have club-branded photo opportunities and ensure that everyone has excellent Wi-Fi and cell phone reception, as that is your opportunity for referrals.

Applying our nightclub knowledge to a boutique childcare facility resulted in an initial assessment of the moments of peak happiness. The two moments were right when the child is accepted into the program and a few months postenrollment when the child has developed his or her first tangible skill.

The euphoria of the first moment was amplified by creating a stronger sense of acceptance scarcity and competition, just like the arbitrary line queue outside a nightclub. This set the stage for the second moment of peak happiness, which was accompanied by an automated email that went out asking if there were any other parents they knew of that would benefit from the same phenomenal experience their child was receiving.

By formalizing and automating the referral ask, the facility was flooded with prospective parents that were amazed by the beautiful facility and student-to-teacher ratio (a sales point that was strengthened when they were at 50 percent enrollment). The results were so immediate and effective that we didn't even have to implement referral incentives. By the end of the first semester, they were at 100 percent capacity.

REFERRALS & RETENTION TAKEAWAYS

- The difference between an active referral system and a passive referral system is often the singular difference between a static company and a high-growth company.
- Increasing client retention increases Customer Lifetime Value, which in turn allows a business to justify spending more money on customer acquisition. This opens up new customer acquisition channels that are otherwise unaffordable.
- Testimonial formula: [Specific End Result or Benefit the Customer Received] + [Specific Period of Time] + [Accompanied Customer Emotion] + [Customer Name with Relevant Stats].
- Preempt negative commentary through satisfaction surveys and other internal feedback forms.
- Don't ignore negative commentary on review sites and social media; control the conversation.
- How to handle negative commentary: For a negative truth, admit, apologize, and promote the opposite; for a negative lie, state that the comment is inaccurate or invalid, and substantiate your comment.
- Retention improvements are particularly potent for early-stage companies and mature companies that have not recently spent time optimizing the retention process.
- The two primary categories of active referral systems are financial and in-kind.

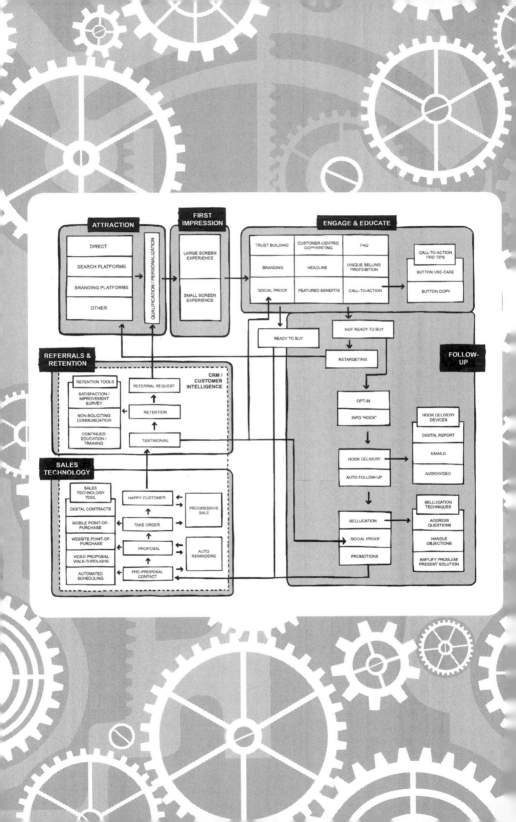

CONCLUSION

Silicon Valley's ability to produce rapid and sustained growth was kept "secret" because everyone was so busy making money that no one stopped to write everything down in one organized framework, until now.

Silicon Valley has transcended the definition of a physical place and has become an ideology that is being propagated to every industry in every corner of the globe. The rise of the Roman Empire can be viewed as the historical analog for the dissemination of Silicon Valley ideology. In Rome, technological advances in agriculture and weaponry were institutionalized in the form of government and philosophy. What occurred was a "Romanization" of the rest of the world in the form of Roman governance in far-off cities and a Roman intellectual enlightenment. Similarly,

Silicon Valley is sprouting derivatives in far-off lands such as Silicon Oasis of Dubai, Thames Valley of England, and Silicon Gulf of the Philippines, evangelizing the disruptive "do more with less" operating system called growth hacking. Now that you understand the philosophy and framework of growth hacking, you have the power to build your own empire.

THE WHOLE IS OTHER THAN THE SUM OF THE PARTS

With the ASP™ blueprint in hand, you are equipped to identify the points of greatest opportunity. Depending on your current situation, the opportunity may come in the form of amplifying your points of strength; perhaps that means formalizing and incentivizing a referral program. Alternatively, opportunity may come in the form of remedying an ailing ASP™ weakness; perhaps that means implementing a way to capture interested prospects and follow up with them over time. When all components are in place, the proverbial flywheel will begin to gain momentum, and your automated ASP™ growth-hacking engine will take you further than any individual component in isolation.

In each chapter we drew parallels from existing analog "real world" processes and showed you the digital manifestation. The purpose behind this approach was to take your existing paradigm, inject it with digital technology, and reassemble it within a framework that capitalizes on the best high-growth practices Silicon Valley has to offer. The resulting ASP™ is a systemized way of growth hacking *any* business. You can now grow your business and expand your profits without working eighteen-hour days, hiring tons of new staff, and waking up every night with migraines. The ASP™ will empower you to do the following:

ASP™ SUMMARY

1. **ATTRACT** thousands of interested new leads.
2. Create a powerful **FIRST IMPRESSION** to set the tone for a consistent, personalized, and professional experience with your company.
3. **ENGAGE & EDUCATE** your prospects so they have all the information they need to feel comfortable buying from you.
4. Implement a seamless **FOLLOW-UP** process so that no business slips through the cracks and your company is always top-of-mind.
5. Use **SALES TECHNOLOGY** to more efficiently close sales, upsell, and cross-sell products and services.
6. Generate high-value **REFERRALS** while **RETAINING** existing clients.

While each individual component of the ASP™ is valuable in isolation, they're all priceless when combined. The whole-is-other-than-the-sum-of-the-parts result is now within your reach. As the saying goes, begin with the end in mind. The end for you is a high-margin, sustainably growing business that is spitting out cash like a jackpot-winning slot machine in Las Vegas. This machine is built with your own hands, your own ingenuity, and it serves as a perpetually productive fountain of freedom.

THE WHY THAT MAKES US CRY

This book is our legacy. It's years of experiential lessons learned, distilled with a vintner's patience and love of craft into a succinct and actionable manuscript. As active growth-hacking practitioners, we wrote this book in the dark predawn hours before the workday and when our peers were watching football on the weekends. You were the motivation for this sacrifice, and it brings us immeasurable joy and fulfillment to be able to share what we have learned with you.

The "why that makes us cry" is you. Our life's work thus far has been encapsulated in a document that can be consumed by you in a matter of hours. In a relatively short period of time, you have accumulated enough working knowledge of growth hacking to accomplish amazing things. By coupling the growth-hacking expertise with your industry expertise, you have a powerful concoction of skill sets that has never before existed in your field of work. You are destined to achieve greatness, and when you do, we'd love to hear your story of success.

On the path to extraordinary achievement, armed with Silicon Valley's best kept secret, and fueled by your "why," you will be an indomitable, unstoppable force. Take a look at what you wrote down for the "why that makes you cry" in chapter 0. Let your "why" soak into your subconscious so it becomes the psychological weapon that you wield when the fickle and fearful conscious wages war. By swiftly defeating the treasonous temptations your conscious dangles before you, whether that be the fear of the unknown, the fear of missing out, or some other passing distraction, you will resolutely stay your course destined for extraordinary success.

SUCCESS IS A PROCESS, NOT A DESTINATION

"It's good to have an end to journey toward, but it's the journey that matters in the end."

—URSULA K. LE GUIN

As someone who had the commitment to complete this book, you have already proven yourself as an achiever.

While this has and will continue to set you apart from your peers, you also need to remain aware of the trade-offs that espouse your commitment to completion. Money is a renewable resource, but time irrevocably and mercilessly marches forward. Taking time to enjoy the journey and celebrate the milestones will refill, refuel, and recharge your energy on your path to extraordinary success.

Go confidently and go now. You will develop the requisite growth-hacking skills as the journey demands. Your path will reveal itself with each passing step. Yes, you will fail at times, but when you move fast, you fail forward. Yes, you will have doubt cast shadows across your path, but your "why" will shatter shadows with faith's light.

"IT'S GOOD TO HAVE AN END TO JOURNEY TOWARD, BUT IT'S THE JOURNEY THAT MATTERS IN THE END."

— URSULA K. LE GUIN

ABOUT THE AUTHORS

ABOUT RAYMOND FONG

Raymond Fong acquired his undergraduate degree in engineering from Harvey Mudd College. While working in the aerospace industry as a systems engineer on top-secret government projects, he obtained his graduate degree in engineering from the University of Southern California. After five years in engineering, Raymond discovered his passion lay in marketing and consulting. He went on to establish himself as a recognized expert in the internet marketing arena. Since 2005, he has coached, mentored, and trained tens of thousands of business owners around the world. In 2014, Raymond cofounded a growth-hacking consulting agency, Deviate Labs, with Chad Riddersen.

ABOUT CHAD RIDDERSEN

Chad Riddersen graduated from the University of Southern California at the age of twenty. After spending a year at Deloitte, consulting for Fortune 500 companies, Chad went on to work in investment banking, where he helped growth-stage companies raise capital and get acquired. As an investment banker, Chad raised sixty-seven million dollars for LegalZoom, an online legal-services company, sold a company to American Express, and sold a company to TiVo, among other transactions. After investment banking, Chad began his work as a growth consultant and first worked with Dollar Shave Club, which later was acquired by Unilever for one billion dollars. Chad went on to form a growth-hacking consulting agency, Deviate Labs, in collaboration with Raymond Fong.

ABOUT DEVIATE LABS

The shared thesis that led to the formation of Deviate Labs was that Silicon Valley growth hacking would inevitably change the way all businesses approach marketing. While Deviate Labs has worked and will always work with a stable of high-tech, venture-backed start-ups, the intention from the outset was to apply growth-hacking tactics to traditional, nontech companies. When the first few implementations of Silicon Valley growth-hacking tactics produced wild success, Chad and Raymond underwent a twenty-four-month process of distilling down the many one-off tactics into a documented, repeatable framework for growth. The result was the Automated Sales Process™ (ASP™), the foundation for duplicating exponential, Silicon Valley-style growth.

GROWTH-HACKING TOOLS & RESOURCES

We're often asked what growth-hacking tools we recommend, and our recommendations constantly change as new technologies emerge. As such, we put together a webpage that we update on a regular basis: DeviateLabs.com/Resources